PRAYERS & DECLARATIONS
for the

WOMAN
of GOD

MICHELLE MᶜCLAIN-WALTERS

CHARISMA
HOUSE

PRAYERS AND DECLARATIONS FOR THE WOMAN OF GOD
  by Michelle McClain-Walters
Published by Charisma House
Charisma Media/Charisma House Book Group
600 Rinehart Road
Lake Mary, Florida 32746
www.charismahouse.com

Cover design by Lisa Rae McClure
Design Director: Justin Evans

Visit the author's website at www.michellemcclainwalters.com.

Library of Congress Cataloging-in-Publication Data:
An application to register this book for cataloging has been submitted to the Library of Congress.
International Standard Book Number: 978-1-62999-480-2
E-book ISBN: 978-1-62999-481-9

Portions of this book were previously published by Charisma House as *The Esther Anointing,* ISBN 978-1-62136-587-7, copyright © 2014; *The Deborah Anointing,* ISBN

978-1-62998-606-7, copyright © 2015, *The Anna Anointing*, ISBN 978-1-62998-947-1, copyright © 2017; *The Ruth Anointing*, ISBN 978-1-62999-463-5, copyright © 2018.

18 19 20 21 22—987654321
Printed in the United States of America

CONTENTS

Part III: Outer Transformation

Part IV: Going Deeper

Part V: Becoming a Woman of God

INTRODUCTION

L IFE IS FULL of seasons. Some are difficult, and others are easy. Some are joyful, and others can be full of grief and pain. Some seasons are full of growth and success, and some are a time of God calling you deeper. Wherever you are in life, though, I know that God is there in the midst of it all with you. He has something to speak to you in your current situation, and He has a plan for your future.

This book seeks to help you wherever you are. It talks of different seasons and circumstances women of God experience, with topics ranging from trusting in God to letting go of bitterness to serving others to waging spiritual warfare to becoming a woman of virtue. Each topic includes Scripture to guide you, short one-to-two-sentence declarations for you to proclaim over your life, longer and deeper prayers, and a journaling section for you to write your own prayers and declarations for each different area of life and season.

Each of these components has its own uses in your growth process. Scripture is, of course, the first place you should look as you face a new season of life or an obstacle you must overcome. As 2 Timothy 3:16–17 says, "All Scripture is inspired by God and is profitable for teaching, for reproof, for correction, and for instruction in righteousness, that the man of God may be complete, thoroughly equipped for every good work." Each topic begins with Scripture that relates because it is the first place we should look, and Scripture should inform the declarations we proclaim and the prayers that we pray. Read these scriptures and think about what they are speaking to your life today, and seek to implement them in your actions, declarations, and prayers.

Next, each section includes several one-to-two-sentence declarations. These are short, but they are powerful! Many of these declarations are birthed out of Scripture itself. What better to proclaim over your life, plans, family, city, and future than the Word of God? Because these declarations are so short, you can memorize them and speak them daily over your life. You could write them down on Post-it Notes and stick them to your mirror to pray over as you prepare for each day. Or you can store them in your phone and set a timer to remind you to make a decree for the day. Or you could put them on index cards in your pocket or purse and pull them out in spare moments to proclaim and pray over your life. Whatever your method is, take these declarations with you. Use them each day as you seek to grow deeper in your relationship with the Father.

Each topic also includes deeper and longer prayers. These are in-depth prayers for each topic. Pieces of them relate to Scripture, and some are simply prayers from my heart that I prayed through something I had to overcome. Take these prayers and pray them yourself. Think these words through, make sure you are praying from your heart, and then take them before the Lord.

Each topic ends with a place for you to write your own declarations and prayers. Take a scripture and turn it into a declaration you can proclaim over your life and your future. Or write your own longer, heartfelt prayers. Or you can do both. This is where you get to be an active participant. You have seen Scripture; you have seen examples of declarations and prayers. Now make them your own. Personalize your declarations and prayers for the exact situation you are in, and pray them out.

You can read this book straight through if you'd like. However, it is made to be useful to you wherever you are. So if you are going through something, find the section that relates to where you are and work through that part first. The book is divided into five parts with more specific topics within each part. You can find a broad subject you are dealing with, such as seeking inner transformation through Christ, and read through each topic in succession. You can also find specific topics that relate to exactly what you are going through today and go through that part only. In other words, this book is yours. Use it in the manner that is most helpful to you as you seek to deepen your relationship with Christ and begin to share Him with those around you.

Part I

DRAWING CLOSE TO GOD

G OD FAVORS WOMEN who commit their lives to ministering to Him—who draw near to Him, worship Him, declare His worth on the earth, meditate on His Word, and access His heart. Ministering to the Lord means loving God with all of our hearts. This is our primary calling, even above ministering to others. Learning to repent, trust God, and abide in Him are keys to remaining close to the Lord, and the prayers and declarations in this section will help you do just that.

When we draw close to God, we will serve and work from a place of love and not for the sake of works or performance. Many times we can develop a works mentality and lose our sense of self-worth. As we spend time with the Lord, He will bring breakthrough to our hearts, and we will see ourselves in the light of His glory.

Ministering to the Lord is not burdensome—it is a privilege and honor. It is key to developing your identity; it is key to unlocking your destiny. Psalm 16:11 says, "You will make known to me the path of life; in Your presence is fullness of joy; at Your right hand there are pleasures for evermore." If you're facing confusion regarding who you are and what you're designed to do with your life, try ministering to the Lord. As you consecrate yourself to God and spend time declaring His name and your love for Him, He will show you the path of life.

REPENT

Scripture

Have mercy on me, O God, according to Your loving-kindness; according to the abundance of Your compassion, blot out my transgressions. Wash me thoroughly from my iniquity, and cleanse me from my sin. For I acknowledge my transgressions, and my sin is ever before me. Against You, You only, have I sinned, and done this evil in Your sight, so that You are justified when You speak, and You are blameless when You judge. I was brought forth in iniquity, and in sin my mother conceived me. You desire truth in the inward parts, and in the hidden part You make me to know wisdom. Purify me with hyssop, and I will be clean; wash me, and I will be whiter than snow. Make me to hear joy and gladness, that the bones that You have broken may rejoice. Hide Your face from my sins, and blot out all my iniquities. Create in me a clean heart, O God, and renew a right spirit within me. Do not cast me away from Your presence, and do not take Your Holy Spirit from me. Restore to me the joy of Your salvation, and uphold me with Your willing spirit.
—Psalm 51:1–12

He who covers his sins will not prosper, but whoever confesses and forsakes them will have mercy.

—PROVERBS 28:13

Rend your heart, and not your garments; return to the LORD your God, for He is gracious and merciful, slow to anger, and abounding in steadfast love; and He relents from punishing.

—JOEL 2:13

Jesus answered them, "Those who are well do not need a physician, but those who are sick. I have not come to call the righteous, but sinners to repentance."

—LUKE 5:31–32

If we confess our sins, He is faithful and just to forgive us our sins and cleanse us from all unrighteousness.

—1 JOHN 1:9

DECLARATIONS

I will open my heart and spirit for the Lord's voice, asking Him to convict me of any sin in my life.

When I experience godly sorrow, I will rejoice, knowing it will lead to repentance (2 Cor. 7:10).

The Lord is gracious and merciful; He will show me this as I repent and turn to Him.

As I acknowledge my sin and repent, I will be cleansed and renewed.

If I am found in Christ, the Lord will forgive me and make me new (2 Cor. 5:17).

The Lord came to heal the sick, to call the sinners to repentance; I will answer the call.

If I confess my sin, the Lord is faithful and just to forgive me my sin and cleanse me from all unrighteousness (1 John 1:9).

PRAYERS

Father, I come boldly to the throne of grace to obtain mercy and find grace in time of need. I ask that You will have mercy on me according to Your loving-kindness and tender mercies. Blot out my transgressions and wash me thoroughly from my sin. Lord, I ask that You create in me a clean heart and renew a righteous spirit within me. I repent of [say what you need to repent of]. *Lord, I ask that You forgive me. I acknowledge my sin, and I ask that You purge me with hyssop and cleanse me from sin. Let joy and gladness return to my heart. In Jesus's name I pray.*

Father, I ask that You will release the spirit of conviction upon the hearts of men once again. Let there be a deep conviction of sin. Many have become politically correct, leaving the truth of the gospel. I pray that leaders will preach the truth of Your Word once

again. Let the anointing of the refiner's fire be released in Your church. Purify and burn out anything in our hearts that is not like You. Your Word says that the product of godly sorrow is repentance. Lord, I pray that the body of Christ will come to true repentance, confession, and action. I pray that true spiritual brokenness would return to the church. Let there be a returning to fasting, weeping, and mourning. Let the pastors in my nation preach messages that encourage true repentance.

YOUR TURN

Use the space below to write out your own prayers and declarations.

ABIDE

SCRIPTURE

You shall seek Me and find Me, when you shall search
for Me with all your heart.

—JEREMIAH 29:13

Remain in Me, as I also remain in you. As the branch
cannot bear fruit by itself, unless it remains in the vine,
neither can you, unless you remain in Me. I am the
vine, you are the branches. He who remains in Me, and
I in him, bears much fruit. For without Me you can do
nothing. If a man does not remain in Me, he is thrown
out as a branch and withers. And they gather them
and throw them into the fire, and they are burned. If
you remain in Me, and My words remain in you, you
will ask whatever you desire, and it shall be done for
you. My Father is glorified by this, that you bear much
fruit; so you will be My disciples. As the Father loved
Me, I also loved you. Remain in My love.

—JOHN 15:4–9

I have been crucified with Christ. It is no longer I who
live, but Christ who lives in me. And the life I now
live in the flesh, I live by faith in the Son of God, who
loved me and gave Himself for me.

—GALATIANS 2:20

7

DECLARATIONS

I will abide in the Lord, and as I do so, I will grow in fruitfulness.

I will seek the Lord's face continually. As I seek the Lord's thoughts, He will fill my heart, mind, and soul with His perspective about my life.

The Lord is the vine, and I am the branch, dependent on Him and His nourishment.

I can do nothing without the Lord, so I will stay in His presence.

I will turn to the Lord and seek His presence, for I need Him in my life.

I no longer live in the strength of my flesh, but Christ lives in me.

The Lord will lead me along the paths of righteousness.

PRAYER

I believe Your Word. You are the vine, and I am the branch. I abide and remain in You all of the days of my life. Without You I can do nothing. I need You and Your presence in my life. Lead me and guide me by Your Spirit. I want to have fruit that remains in my life. I want to have godly character as I abide in You. Show me Your ways. Lead me in the paths of righteousness for Your name's sake.

YOUR TURN

Use the space below to write out your own prayers and declarations.

FIND REDEMPTION AND RESTORATION

SCRIPTURE

He sent redemption to His people; He has commanded His covenant forever; holy and fearful is His name.

—PSALM 111:9

Let Israel wait for the LORD! For mercy is found with the LORD; with Him is great redemption.

—PSALM 130:7

Therefore repent and be converted, that your sins may be wiped away, that times of refreshing may come from the presence of the Lord, and that He may send the One who previously was preached to you, Jesus Christ, whom the heavens must receive until the time of restoring what God spoke through all His holy prophets since the world began.

—ACTS 3:19–21

In Him we have redemption through His blood and the forgiveness of sins according to the riches of His grace.

—EPHESIANS 1:7

DECLARATIONS

I will wash myself and prepare for the redemption of the Lord (Eph. 5:26–27).

I will seek sanctification from the Lord.

I will seek anointing from the Holy Spirit in my search for redemption.

God the Father will serve as my Redeemer, and He will separate me from things keeping me from where I should be.

God will cover me and place me under His protection.

The Lord will restore me.

I will sit at the Redeemer's feet waiting for instruction.

PRAYER

Father, I humble myself under Your mighty hand. You are just and righteous. I have no righteousness of my own. I place my life in Your hand. Lord, I ask that You cleanse my heart by the washing of Your Word. Change my heart as You change my circumstances. I draw my life from You. I draw my strength from You. I draw my peace from You.

YOUR TURN

Use the space below to write out your own prayers and declarations.

BECOME A LIVING SACRIFICE

SCRIPTURE

I urge you therefore, brothers, by the mercies of God, that you present your bodies as a living sacrifice, holy, and acceptable to God, which is your reasonable service of worship.

—ROMANS 12:1

What? Do you not know that your body is the temple of the Holy Spirit, who is in you, whom you have received from God, and that you are not your own? You were bought with a price. Therefore glorify God in your body and in your spirit, which are God's.

—1 CORINTHIANS 6:19–20

Therefore be imitators of God as beloved children. Walk in love, as Christ loved us and gave Himself for us as a fragrant offering and a sacrifice to God.

—EPHESIANS 5:1–2

DECLARATIONS

I will submit myself to the Lord as an act of submission.

I will be a living sacrifice to the Lord and submit myself to holiness as an act of worship.

My body is a temple of the Holy Spirit; I will live unto Him and glorify Him with my body and my life.

I will not live as the world does; instead I will be transformed by the Lord and follow His will for my life.

I will love the Father, not the things of the world (1 John 2:15–16).

I will live my life as a sacrifice unto the Lord.

I will continually humble myself before the mighty hand of God.

PRAYER

Lord, I present my body to You as a living sacrifice. I draw nigh to You with my entire heart. I give myself to You. I want to be holy and acceptable to You. My life is in Your hands. I give You my heart and all of my pains and disappointments. Create in me a clean heart, and renew a right, steadfast spirit within me. Lord, take me to the mount of change. I want to be transformed into Your image. Make me like You. Show me why You created me.

YOUR TURN

Use the space below to write out your own prayers and declarations.

CONSECRATE YOURSELF

SCRIPTURE

Consecrate yourselves today to the LORD, that He may bestow a blessing on you this day.

—EXODUS 32:29

Consecrate yourselves therefore, and be holy, for I am the LORD your God. You shall keep my statutes, and do them; I am the LORD who sanctifies you.

—LEVITICUS 20:7–8

You shall be holy unto Me; for I the LORD am holy and have separated you from other peoples, that you should be Mine.

—LEVITICUS 20:26

For you are a holy people to the LORD your God. The LORD your God has chosen you to be His special people, treasured above all peoples who are on the face of the earth.

—DEUTERONOMY 7:6

But you are a chosen race, a royal priesthood, a holy nation, a people for God's own possession, so that you may declare the goodness of Him who has called you out of darkness into His marvelous light.

—1 PETER 2:9

DECLARATION

I will dedicate my life to the service of the Lord.

I will consecrate myself to the Lord so that He may give a blessing (Exod. 32:29).

As one who is set apart, I will practice the presence of the Lord in my daily life.

I will separate myself from the world and instead spend hours seeking the Lord and His presence through prayer.

God will set me apart for His divine purpose.

PRAYER

Father, I dedicate my life to You. I submit my will to Your will. As Jesus prayed in Mark 14:36, not my will but Your will be done in my life. My desire is to live in total obedience to Your will. Lord, I ask that You work in me to will and do of Your good pleasure. Father, I trust You with the details of my life. I have plans, thoughts, ideas, and visions for my life, but in this moment I lay them all at Your feet. Abba, I trust You. I believe You know what's best for me. Remove any relationships, habits, or projects from my life that are not in Your perfect will for my life. I give myself completely to You. I am Yours.

YOUR TURN

Use the space below to write out your own prayers and declarations.

WAIT ON THE LORD

SCRIPTURE

Wait on the LORD; be strong, and may your heart be stout; wait on the LORD.

—PSALM 27:14

I wait for the LORD, with bated breath I wait; I long for His Word! My soul waits for the Lord, more than watchmen for the morning, more than watchmen for the morning.

—PSALM 130:5–6

But those who wait for the LORD [who expect, look for, and hope in Him] will gain new strength and renew their power; they will lift up their wings [and rise up close to God] like eagles [rising toward the sun]; they will run and not become weary, they will walk and not grow tired.

—ISAIAH 40:31, AMP

Therefore be patient, brothers, until the coming of the Lord. Notice how the farmer waits for the precious fruit of the earth and is patient with it until he receives the early and late rain. You also be patient. Establish your hearts, for the coming of the Lord is drawing near.

—JAMES 5:7–8

DECLARATIONS

I will be patient and wait on the Lord.

I will continually wait for God (Hosea 12:6).

Each period of waiting will be a time of refreshing and renewal for me.

I will grow in strength and patience as I wait.

I will watch for the Lord with expectant hope while I wait (Ps. 5:3).

I believe I will see the goodness of the Lord, and I will be strong as I wait for Him (Ps. 27:13–14; 31:24).

PRAYER

I will wait for You, Jesus. You're the strength of my life. Lord, I ask that You renew my strength as the eagle's. Let this be a season of refreshing and renewal in my life. I believe that You give power to the weak, and to those who have no might, You increase strength. I receive Your divine empowerment in my life. I break all discouragement and weakness from my life. I decree that I am strong in the Lord and in the power of His might! I will not be weary, nor will I faint! I look to the hills from which comes my help. My help comes from the Lord!

YOUR TURN

Use the space below to write out your own prayers and declarations.

_____

_____

_____

_____

_____

_____

_____

_____

_____

_____

_____

_____

_____

_____

_____

_____

_____

_____

_____

TRUST GOD

Scripture

Those who know Your name will put their trust in You, for You, Lord, have not forsaken those who seek You.

—Psalm 9:10

Trust in Him at all times; you people, pour out your heart before Him; God is a shelter for us.

—Psalm 62:8

Trust in the Lord with all your heart, and lean not on your own understanding; in all your ways acknowledge Him, and He will direct your paths.

—Proverbs 3:5–6

Declarations

I will trust the Lord and His plans and purposes for me (Prov. 3:5–6).

I will trust God's heart for me, even if I don't understand.

I will open myself up to relationship with God, confiding in Him, because I know I can trust in Him (Ps. 62:8).

I am blessed because I put my trust in the Lord (Jer. 17:7).

I will trust in the Lord's sovereign care over every aspect of my life.

When I am afraid, I will trust in the Lord (Ps. 56:3).

I trust that the Lord will deliver me (2 Cor. 1:10).

PRAYER

Lord, Your Word says to trust You at all times (Ps. 62:8). Father, I ask that You would release the grace to trust. Many times I trust in my abilities, my reasonings, and my understanding. Lord, I repent for carnal thinking. I repent for walking by sight instead of walking by faith. I repent for trusting in the arm of flesh. I repent for trusting men instead of Your love for me. Lord, from this day forward I acknowledge You in all my ways, and I believe You will direct my path. Let Your grace come upon me to communicate with You. I desire life-giving intimacy with You, Lord. Let Your words direct my path. As I worship You, let Your words fill my mind, soul, and spirit. Thank You, Lord, for directions, fruitfulness, and victories birthed from constant contact with You.

YOUR TURN

Use the space below to write out your own prayers and declarations.

SUBMIT TO GOD

SCRIPTURE

Your kingdom come; Your will be done on earth, as it is in heaven.

—MATTHEW 6:10

Therefore submit yourselves to God. Resist the devil, and he will flee from you.

—JAMES 4:7

DECLARATIONS

I will submit to the Lord and His plans, just as Christ did (Luke 22:42).

I will yield to God's call on my life and submit myself to Him.

I will humble myself so I can submit myself to the Lord and His will.

I will deliberately and intentionally submit myself to the Lord.

I will submit to the Lord by giving my life to Him and being a sacrifice, by working for His glory, by serving His people, by spending time in His Word, and by loving my neighbor.

PRAYER

Father, Your Word says in James 4:7, "Submit your-selves to God. Resist the devil, and he will flee from you." I repent for any form of rebellion that has been operating in my life. Reveal areas of rebellion in my life. I renounce all unteachable spirits in my life. I renounce all self-willed demons connected to Jezebel. I renounce and break off any spirits of stubbornness and pride operating in my life. Your Word says that rebellion is as the sin of witchcraft. I release myself from generational rebellion that leads to witchcraft. I break off all spirits of hardness of heart. I break off all spirits of stiff-necked pride. I humble myself under Your mighty hand. I submit to Your authority in my life. Jesus, You are my Lord and my King. Let the increase of Your government and peace reign in my life.

YOUR TURN

Use the space below to write out your own prayers and declarations.

WAGE WAR THROUGH WORSHIP

SCRIPTURE

After talking it over with the people, Jehoshaphat appointed a choir for GOD; dressed in holy robes, they were to march ahead of the troops, singing, Give thanks to GOD, His love never quits.

—2 CHRONICLES 20:21, THE MESSAGE

He who dwells in the secret place of the Most High shall remain stable and fixed under the shadow of the Almighty [Whose power no foe can withstand].

—PSALM 91:1, AMPC

Let the high praises of God be in their mouth, and a two-edged sword in their hand; to execute vengeance upon the heathen, and punishments upon the people; to bind their kings with chains, and their nobles with fetters of iron; to execute upon them the judgment written; this honour have all his saints. Praise ye the LORD.

—PSALM 149:6–9, KJV

Believe me, woman, the time is coming when you Samaritans will worship the Father neither here at this mountain nor there in Jerusalem. You worship guessing in the dark; we Jews worship in the clear light of day. God's way of salvation is made available through the Jews. But the time is coming—it has, in fact, come—when what you're called will not matter and where you go to worship will not matter.

It's who you are and the way you live that count before God. Your worship must engage your spirit in the pursuit of truth. That's the kind of people the Father is out looking for: those who are simply and honestly themselves before him in their worship. God is sheer being itself—Spirit. Those who worship him must do it out of their very being, their spirits, their true selves, in adoration.

—John 4:21–24, The Message

DECLARATIONS

Being a passionate worshipper of the Lord will prepare me to be a warrior; it will prepare me for my destiny in the Lord.

I will live a life of worship and praise that will usher in the presence of God.

I will worship the Lord in every circumstance, even and especially while fighting a battle.

By praising and worshipping, I am participating in spiritual warfare against my enemies.

PRAYER

Lord, in the midst of my trial, I will worship You. When I don't understand the "whys" of life, I still say You are blameless and just. Jesus, You are my champion. You are faithful and true. The foundations of Your throne are righteousness and justice. I put on the breastplate of righteousness to guard my heart from accusing You. After I've done all to stand, I will stand and lift my hands and declare You are worthy! You are worthy to receive blessings and honor, glory and power! This is my warfare to bless You, Lord, at all times. Your praises shall continually be in my mouth! I press in to Your presence, where I find peace that surpasses all understanding.

YOUR TURN

Use the space below to write out your own prayers and declarations.

_____

_____

_____

_____

_____

_____

_____

_____

PRAY AND FAST

SCRIPTURE

Then all the children of Israel, all the people, went up to Bethel where they wept and sat before the LORD. They fasted that day until evening and offered burnt offerings and peace offerings before the LORD. The children of Israel asked the LORD... "Should we go out again to wage war with our brother-tribesmen the Benjamites, or should we not?" The LORD said, "Go up, for tomorrow I will give them into your hands."

—JUDGES 20:26–28

I humbled my soul with fasting; and my prayer returns to my own heart.

—PSALM 35:13

Is this not the fast that I have chosen: to loose the bonds of wickedness, to undo the heavy burdens, to let the oppressed go free, and break every yoke?

—ISAIAH 58:6

But this kind does not go out except by prayer and fasting.

—MATTHEW 17:21

The end of all things is near. Therefore be solemn and sober so you can pray.

—1 PETER 4:7

29

Declarations

Just as Jesus was strengthened by fasting to withstand temptation, so will I be (Luke 4:14, 18).

I will fast and pray to soften my heart and ready it for repentance.

I will receive breakthrough in my life through prayer and fasting (Ezra 8:21, 31).

I will pray without ceasing (1 Thess. 5:17).

Prayer

Father, as I humble myself with prayer and fasting, I believe that You will break every yoke of bondage in my life. I believe that during this time of fasting things in my life will turn around for the better. Father, I believe that during this time of fasting I will access the spirit of wisdom and revelation. Lord, I need direction in my life. I need answers to my prayers so I can quiet my soul with fasting to hear Your wisdom. As I ask You specific questions, I believe You will give me specific directions. Awaken my spiritual ears to hear Your still, small voice.

Your Turn

Use the space below to write out your own prayers and declarations.

GIVE GLORY TO GOD

SCRIPTURE

Not unto us, O Lord, not unto us, but unto Your name give glory, for the sake of Your mercy, and for the sake of Your truth.

—Psalm 115:1

Therefore, whether you eat, or drink, or whatever you do, do it all to the glory of God.

—1 Corinthians 10:31

You are worthy, O Lord, to receive glory and honor and power; for You have created all things, and by Your will they exist and were created.

—Revelation 4:11

DECLARATIONS

My hands, feet, and mouth were formed to minister to and worship the Lord. I was created to bless Him, and that is how I will spend my life.

I will declare the Lord's worth on the earth.

I will give the glory to God alone.

Everything I do, all of my work and my play, will be for God's glory (1 Cor. 10:31).

God is worthy of glory (Rev. 4:11).

There is no one like the Lord.

PRAYERS

Lord, I give You the glory due Your name. All blessing and honor and glory and power be unto You! Lord, You are great and greatly to be praised! Your greatness is unsearchable. There is no one like You. I bless You and magnify Your name. You are great, and You are a miracle worker. Let all creation bow down before You! I declare You are worthy! You are worthy to receive honor. Holy are You, Lord! Faithful are You, Lord! You are merciful, gracious, and slow to anger. Lord, You are good to me, and I love You with all of my heart and soul and all that I know. My soul makes its boast in You. Be exalted in the heavens. Be magnified on the earth. Power belongs to You, God, and You rule and reign on the earth! Let Your ways be known on the earth and Your salvation among the nations!

I want to see You high and lifted up. Lord, I want to know You. In Your presence is fullness of joy. Lord, show me the path of life. Lord, my soul thirsts for You. Come, Holy Spirit, and quench my thirst. I seek Your face. I long to see Your power and Your glory. I want to see You like Isaiah saw You, high and lifted up (Isa. 6:1).

God, give me revelation of who You are. Remove the scales from my eyes. I long to see humanity from Your perspective. Lead me and guide me. I want to be sent from Your presence. Take the coal from Your heavenly altar and cleanse me from any iniquity and sin that would hinder my call. In Jesus's name I pray. Amen.

YOUR TURN

Use the space below to write out your own prayers and declarations.

Part II

INNER TRANSFORMATION

I F YOU REMEMBER the story of Esther, you know her journey to greatness and influence did not happen overnight. She did not arrive in the palace one day and have the king fall in love with her and make her queen the next. She had to endure a beautifying process mandated by Persian culture that included six months in oil of myrrh and six months in spices and ointments. Every young girl in the harem had to go through this process before she could even approach the king.

Just as Esther endured a physical beautifying process to prepare for her assignment as queen, so must we go through a spiritual beautifying process as God prepares us for our destinies and purposes. The refining of our characters is essential to God's plan for our lives. God cannot use a proud woman (or man). The preparation process God takes us through presses and purges out impurities of the heart and spirit, such as pride, rebellion, selfishness, and bitterness, so we can be pliable in the hands of the Lord to follow His lead to fulfill our purposes. We can't be an effective vessel with baggage weighing on us, affecting our ability to hear and obey God.

We can have far-reaching influence and a legacy that

spans cultures and generations, just as Esther did. But we must first submit to the beautification and purification process of the Holy Spirit. Use the prayers and declarations in this section to allow the Holy Spirit to transform you from the inside out. His refining will purge out of us the things that will hinder us from being the women God has called us to be and infuse into us the fragrant character of God. As we begin to authentically display the attributes of a godly woman, we will find favor to fulfill our assignments. We will find the scepter being extended to us without limit to every place our feet should tread.

PERSEVERE IN FAITH

SCRIPTURE

I believe I will see the goodness of the LORD in the land of the living.

—PSALM 27:13

Jesus said to them, "Because of your unbelief. For truly I say to you, if you have faith as a grain of mustard seed, you will say to this mountain, 'Move from here to there,' and it will move. And nothing will be impossible for you."

—MATTHEW 17:20

Jesus said, "If you can believe, all things are possible to him who believes."

—MARK 9:23

I have fought a good fight, I have finished my course, and I have kept the faith.

—2 TIMOTHY 4:7

My brothers, count it all joy when you fall into diverse temptations, knowing that the trying of your faith develops patience. But let patience perfect its work, that you may be perfect and complete, lacking nothing.

—JAMES 1:2–4

Declarations

I will not lose hope or become bitter; instead I will persevere and see the goodness of the Lord.

Through persevering in faith, I have hope for my future.

Even in uncertainty, I will trust the Father.

I am a woman of faith; I stand on the promises of God and trust in His Word.

I walk by faith and not by sight.

I believe God to fulfill my destiny.

I commit my ways unto Him, and He will perfect everything that concerns me (Ps. 138:8).

I am the righteousness of God through Christ Jesus. I live by faith.

I will look to the Author of my life for direction and guidance, trusting Him to know what is best.

I will be faithful with what God says today.

I will trust the Lord with all of my tomorrows.

Prayer

Father, I believe that You love me and will take care of me as You promise in Your Word. I lift up my eyes of faith and look to You, the Author of my life. I cast my cares on You, for You care for me. I believe You will show up and take care of me. I am assured that You will not abandon me. I trust Your plans to give me the future I hoped for. Lord, fill my mind with Your thoughts toward me. I put on the helmet of hope. I shut down the voice of despair. Let my mind and heart be filled with Your precious thoughts for my life.

YOUR TURN

Use the space below to write out your own prayers and declarations.

_____

_____

_____

_____

_____

_____

_____

_____

_____

_____

_____

_____

_____

_____

_____

_____

SEEK HOPE

SCRIPTURE

Why are you cast down, O my soul? And why are you disquieted in me? Hope in God, for I will yet thank Him for the help of His presence. O my God, my soul is cast down within me; therefore I will remember You from the land of Jordan, and of the Hermon, from the hill of Mizar. Deep calls to deep at the noise of Your waterfalls; all Your waves and Your billows passed over me. Yet the LORD will command His lovingkindness in the daytime, and in the night His song will be with me, a prayer to the God of my life.

—PSALM 42:5–8

But I will hope continually, and will praise You yet more and more.

—PSALM 71:14, NKJV

O Israel, hope in the LORD; for with the LORD there is mercy, and with Him is abundant redemption.

—PSALM 130:7, NKJV

Blessed is the man who trusts in the LORD, and whose hope is the LORD.

—JEREMIAH 17:7

I'll show up and take care of you as I promised and bring you back home. I know what I'm doing. I have it all planned out—plans to take care of you, not abandon you, plans to give you the future you hope for.

—Jeremiah 29:10–11, The Message

We know that all things work together for good to those who love God, to those who are called according to His purpose.

—Romans 8:28

Rejoice in hope, be patient in suffering, persevere in prayer.

—Romans 12:12

Now may the God of hope fill you with all joy and peace in believing, so that you may abound in hope, through the power of the Holy Spirit.

—Romans 15:13

So that by two unchangeable things [His promise and His oath] in which it is impossible for God to lie, we who have fled [to Him] for refuge would have strong encouragement and indwelling strength to hold tightly to the hope set before us. This hope [this confident assurance] we have as an anchor of the soul [it cannot slip and it cannot break down under whatever pressure bears upon it]—a safe and steadfast hope that enters within the veil [of the heavenly temple, that most Holy Place in which the very presence of God dwells].

—Hebrews 6:18–19, amp

Therefore, prepare your minds for action, keep sober in spirit, fix your hope completely on the grace to be brought to you at the revelation of Jesus Christ.

—1 Peter 1:13, nasb

Declarations

The hope of Christ is the anchor for my soul.

God is working things together for my good.

God's power is available to help me overcome hopeless situations.

I break the spirit of hopelessness off of my life in the name of Jesus.

I choose to believe that I will see the goodness of the Lord in the land of the living (Ps. 27:13).

I choose to hope, even in the midst of life's hard situations.

I am an overcomer.

I will rejoice in hope.

I will have patience in testing and trials.

I will continue to relentlessly pray to the God of my salvation.

Prayers

God of hope, fill me with all joy and peace. I will trust in You with my whole heart, leaning not on my own understanding. I believe that I will abound in hope by the power of the Holy Ghost. I rebuke all feelings of hope deferred. I will not allow my heart to be weighed down and depressed. By faith I will lift up my voice and praise You. I believe that in the fullness of time my desires will be fulfilled. I will be strong and take heart because I put my hope in You, Lord.

Lord, You are close to the brokenhearted and save those who are crushed in spirit. I admit that I am disappointed. I come boldly without reservation or hesitation to Your throne to obtain mercy and find grace to help in my time of need. I need Your grace to continue. Let Your presence engulf me. Be my shield and exceedingly great reward. I believe in Your saving, delivering power. You are my Savior and will rescue me.

I will not let the devil steal my expectation. I know that surely there is a future for me, so my expectation will not be cut off. I will not settle for less than what You have promised me. I seize the hope that is set before me. I trust in the Lord with all of my heart and lean not on my own understanding. I will not allow my expectation to be cut off by fear, doubt, unbelief, or time.

Lord, my hope is in You! You are my Lord, my strength, and the hope of my salvation. I trust Your Word. I am blessed and highly favored. Your banner over me is love. I run into Your presence and I am safe.

Father, I will hope in You. I will live righteously and serve You with the oil of gladness. I decree that every wicked plot and plan against my life shall be cut off. I cancel every wicked assignment against my life. I will praise Your holy name forever. I partake of Your mercies; they are new every morning. Your love never fails, and Your mercy endures forever.

I am blessed because I put my trust in the Lord. I will not trust in the arm of flesh because my hope, expectation, and confidence is in You, my Lord. I will not let my hope be cut off. I will hope continually in You.

I thank You, Lord, that You have mercy and grace in Your heart for me. I will continually bless You and praise You. Your Word is true. You cannot lie. You will fulfill the desire of every living thing. Lord, I thank You that You open Your hand and satisfy my desire.

Lord, there are times when I feel I have no hope. Help me to hold fast to my confidence in You. Lord, give me the grace I need to persevere in the face of defeat.

Father, because You cannot lie, I seize the hope that is set before me. I find refuge and strong encouragement in Your presence, and I find indwelling strength to hold tightly by prayer and praise to the hope that is set before me.

I believe Your Word. I thank You, Lord, that You are not like man. You cannot lie. You are a God of integrity. Every word You will bring to pass in my life, every promise. I trust Your love and Your character.

    Your words are an anchor for my soul. You are my refuge and my fortress. I run to You and I am safe. I have an expectation that cannot be shaken. No matter what life tries to throw my way, You are my anchor. Your Word keeps me steadfast, unmovable, and abounding in Your love. I will wait for You and the fulfillment of Your words.

YOUR TURN

Use the space below to write out your own prayers and declarations.

_____

_____

_____

_____

_____

_____

_____

_____

_____

_____

_____

_____

LOVE

SCRIPTURE

But You, O Lord, are a God merciful and gracious, slow to anger and abundant in lovingkindness and truth.

—PSALM 86:15, NASB

I love those who love me, and those who seek me early will find me.

—PROVERBS 8:17

For God so loved the world that He gave His only begotten Son, that whoever believes in Him should not perish, but have eternal life.

—JOHN 3:16

If I speak with the tongues of men and of angels, and have not love, I have become as sounding brass or a clanging cymbal. If I have the gift of prophecy, and understand all mysteries and all knowledge, and if I have all faith, so that I could remove mountains, and have not love, I am nothing. If I give all my goods to feed the poor, and if I give my body to be burned, and have not love, it profits me nothing. Love suffers long and is kind; love envies not; love flaunts not itself and is not puffed up, does not behave itself improperly, seeks not its own, is not easily provoked, thinks no evil; rejoices not in iniquity, but rejoices in the truth; bears all things, believes all things, hopes all things, and endures all things. Love never fails. But if there are prophecies, they shall fail; if there are tongues, they shall cease; and if there is knowledge, it shall vanish. For we know in part, and we prophesy in part. But when that which is perfect comes, then that which is imperfect shall pass away. When I was a child, I spoke as a child, I understood as a child, and I thought as a child. But when I became a man, I put away childish things. For now we see as through a glass, dimly, but then, face to face. Now I know in part, but then I shall know, even as I also am known. So now abide faith, hope, and love, these three. But the greatest of these is love.

—1 CORINTHIANS 13

God is love.

—1 JOHN 4:8

DECLARATIONS

The Lord's love for me will transform me from the inside out.

The Lord loves with a perfect love; I will seek to love others with that same type of love.

Because God first loved me, I love Him (1 John 4:19–21).

God is love, and to know love is to know Him (1 John 4:8).

The Lord's steadfast love is good; I will praise Him for it forever.

Prayer

Lord, I believe Your love never fails. I receive Your unfailing love for me. I decree that love abides in my heart. Perfect love casts out all fear. I will not fear the enemies of my soul because You are with me. I believe that nothing can separate me from Your love. I am fully persuaded that neither death nor life nor angels nor principalities nor powers nor things present nor things to come can separate me from Your love.

Your Turn

Use the space below to write out your own prayers and declarations.

PURSUE WISDOM

The mouth of the righteous utters wisdom, and their tongue speaks justice.

—PSALM 37:30

Does not wisdom cry out, and understanding lift up her voice? She takes her stand on the top of the high hill, beside the way, where the paths meet. She cries out by the gates, at the entry of the city, at the entrance of the doors:

"To you, O men, I call, and my voice is to the sons of men. O you simple ones, understand prudence, and you fools, be of an understanding heart. Listen, for I will speak of excellent things, and from the opening of my lips will come right things; for my mouth will speak truth; wickedness is an abomination to my lips. All the words of my mouth are with righteousness; nothing crooked or perverse is in them. They are all plain to him who understands, and right to those who find knowledge. Receive my instruction, and not silver, and knowledge rather than choice gold; for wisdom is better than rubies, and all the things one may desire cannot be compared with her.

"I, wisdom, dwell with prudence, and find out knowledge and discretion. The fear of the LORD is to hate evil; pride and arrogance and the evil way and the perverse mouth I hate. Counsel is mine, and sound wisdom; I am understanding, I have strength. By me kings reign, and rulers decree justice."

—PROVERBS 8:1–15, NKJV

But the Counselor, the Holy Spirit, whom the Father will send in My name, will teach you everything and remind you of all that I told you.

—JOHN 14:26

But when the Spirit of truth comes, He will guide you into all truth. For He will not speak on His own authority. But He will speak whatever He hears, and He will tell you things that are to come.

—JOHN 16:13

That their hearts may be comforted, being knit together in love, and receive all the riches and assurance of full understanding, and knowledge of the mystery of God, both of the Father and of Christ, in whom are hidden all the treasures of wisdom and knowledge.

—COLOSSIANS 2:1–3

If any of you lacks wisdom, let him ask of God, who gives to all men liberally and without criticism, and it will be given to him.

—JAMES 1:5

But the wisdom that is from above is first pure, then peaceable, gentle, open to reason, full of mercy and good fruits, without partiality, and without hypocrisy.

—JAMES 3:17

DECLARATIONS

I will seek the Lord's wisdom, which is full of mercy and good fruits.

I will seek wisdom of the Lord, and He will provide.

God will provide His wisdom so I can overcome hopeless seasons of life.

Wisdom and revelation are my portion.

Wisdom is found on my lips.

I will speak words of wisdom.

The Lord will provide supernatural wisdom when I ask for it.

The Spirit will give me wisdom in the hidden areas of my heart (Ps. 139:23–24).

The Lord will provide both words of wisdom and directional wisdom to help me follow His will for my life.

I will be armed with wisdom.

I will seek wise counsel, for there is safety there (Prov. 15:22).

PRAYERS

Lord, I ask for the gift of the word of wisdom. I want to be a woman of wisdom who responds to situations under Your divine direction. Let me have supernatural perspective to accomplish Your will in every situation. Give me words of wisdom to apply the knowledge given to me by Your Spirit.

Lord, I pray that You will give me wisdom to rightly judge Your people. Let my heart perceive and understand Your ways. Let me not be deceived by crafty and wicked people. Holy Spirit, I ask that You will lead me into all truth. (See 1 Kings 4:29–30; John 14:26; 16:13.)

Lord, pour out Your wisdom upon me. Put Your words in my mouth. Let my heart be filled with wisdom. Lord, I release over me now a supernatural anointing of wisdom. Let that supernatural awakening to wisdom come—that supernatural dimension to know things I would not know on my own—to know the when, the how, the why, and the what.

Release to me wisdom to influence nations. Give me that supernatural release of wisdom that the apostle Paul prayed about. Let dreams and visions begin to churn in my belly. Let thoughts I have never thought before come to me. Wisdom stands at the gate telling me and commanding me to cry out for discernment. God, give me discernment in finances. God, let me begin to understand the economic system as never before.

Open up Your heart to me, Father. I receive Your supernatural anointing for the spirit of wisdom to come into my life. I know that wisdom is one of the sevenfold spirits of the Holy Ghost that Jesus walked in which caused Him to be able to judge the nations. Release this wisdom to me now in Jesus's name. Amen.

YOUR TURN

Use the space below to write out your own prayers and declarations.

FORGIVE AND SEEK FORGIVENESS

SCRIPTURE

Come now, and let us reason together, says the LORD. Though your sins be as scarlet, they shall be as white as snow; though they be red like crimson, they shall be as wool.

—ISAIAH 1:18

For if you forgive men for their sins, your heavenly Father will also forgive you. But if you do not forgive men for their sins, neither will your Father forgive your sins.

—MATTHEW 6:14–15

Then Peter came to Him and said, "Lord, how often shall I forgive my brother who sins against me? Up to seven times?" Jesus said to him, "I do not say to you up to seven times, but up to seventy times seven."

—MATTHEW 18:21–22

Bear with one another and forgive one another. If anyone has a quarrel against anyone, even as Christ forgave you, so you must do.

—COLOSSIANS 3:13

Their sins and lawless deeds will I remember no more.

—HEBREWS 10:17

If we confess our sins, He is faithful and just to forgive
us our sins and cleanse us from all unrighteousness.

—1 JOHN 1:9

DECLARATIONS

I will forgive as the Lord has forgiven me, and I will do so
again and again.

The Lord will forgive me if I turn to Him and repent.

God will remember my sins no more; I will seek to forgive
myself for them as well.

PRAYER

*Holy Spirit, I acknowledge that I've been hurt. I choose
to forgive and release those who have disappointed and
misused me. I forgive those in authority. I forgive my
parents. I forgive my pastor. I forgive my husband. I
forgive myself. I confess the sin of bitterness and anger.
Let the power of Your blood cleanse me. I release love
and peace to my offenders. Create in me a clean heart
and renew a right spirit within me.*

YOUR TURN

Use the space below to write out your own prayers and
declarations.

FIND PEACE

SCRIPTURE

The LORD will give strength to His people; the LORD will bless His people with peace.

—PSALM 29:11

Deceit is in the heart of those who imagine evil, but to the counselors of peace is joy.

—PROVERBS 12:20

If it is possible, as much as it depends on you, live peaceably with all men.

—ROMANS 12:18

Let the peace of God, to which also you are called in one body, rule in your hearts.

—COLOSSIANS 3:15

And the fruit of righteousness is sown in peace by those who make peace.

—JAMES 3:18

Cast all your care upon Him, because He cares for you.

—1 PETER 5:7

DECLARATIONS

I will seek to live in the peace of the Lord.

The Lord will bless me with His peace (Ps. 29:11).

I will go above and beyond to live at peace with all people (Rom. 12:18).

PRAYERS

Lord, I believe that You will give me beauty for ashes. I receive strength instead of fear of the future. Lord, thank You for saturating my heart with the oil of gladness. I choose to put on the garment of praise instead of the spirit of mourning and heaviness. Your presence brings peace to my soul.

Jesus, You are the Prince of Peace. I speak peace to every raging storm in my life. I speak to the storm of fear. I speak peace to storms of confusion. I speak to my heart and mind. Let the peace that surpasses all reasoning and understanding flood my mind. God of peace, crush Satan under my feet. I cast down every imagination and high thing that exalts itself against the knowledge of God. I repent for evil imaginations. I receive the peace and joy of the Lord. I will not be ruled by worry, fear, or anxiety. I decree that my life is ruled by the God of peace. The God of peace rules in my heart. Let the kingdom of God come in my life. Let righteousness, peace, and joy fill my life.

YOUR TURN

Use the space below to write out your own prayers and declarations.

_____

_____

_____

_____

_____

_____

_____

_____

_____

_____

_____

_____

_____

_____

_____

_____

_____

_____

HUMBLE YOURSELF

SCRIPTURE

If My people, who are called by My name, will humble themselves and pray, and seek My face and turn from their wicked ways, then I will hear from heaven, and will forgive their sin and will heal their land.

—2 CHRONICLES 7:14

He gives His grace [His undeserved favor] to the humble [those who give up self-importance].

—PROVERBS 3:34, AMP

When pride comes, then comes shame; but with the humble is wisdom.

—PROVERBS 11:2

Let nothing be done out of strife or conceit, but in humility let each esteem the other better than himself.

—PHILIPPIANS 2:3

God resists the proud, but gives grace to the humble.

—JAMES 4:6

DECLARATIONS

I will live in humility and seek the face of the Lord; then He will forgive us our sins and heal our land.

I resolve to think of others more than myself.

I will have a humble, grace-filled, and teachable spirit.

I can humble myself before God to receive His favor (Luke 15:11–32).

I will develop humility.

Humble women will be co-laborers with Christ.

PRAYER

Father, we humble ourselves under Your mighty hand. We repent of pride, arrogance, vainglory, and haughtiness. We turn from our wicked ways and turn to You. We seek Your face for wisdom and instruction. We ask You to heal our land. Heal our culture. Deliver us from racism and hatred. Let the spirit of forgiveness and reconciliation fill our hearts. Let Your peace return to our nation. In Jesus's name we pray. Amen.

YOUR TURN

Use the space below to write out your own prayers and declarations.

BE HOLY

SCRIPTURE

For I am the LORD your God. You shall therefore sanctify yourselves, and you shall be holy, for I am holy.

—LEVITICUS 11:44

How shall a young man keep his way pure? By keeping it according to Your word.

—PSALM 119:9

Since we have these promises, beloved, let us cleanse ourselves from all filthiness of the flesh and spirit, perfecting holiness in the fear of God.

—2 CORINTHIANS 7:1

But as He who has called you is holy, so be holy in all your conduct, because it is written, "Be holy, for I am holy."

—1 PETER 1:15–16

DECLARATIONS

I will commit anew to radical holiness and purity, to abstain from evil, and to pursue righteousness.

I choose to be a woman of holiness.

God has not called me to impurity, but to holiness (1 Thess. 4:7).

I will turn my attention to things that are true and pure (Phil. 4:8).

Because the Lord is holy, I will be holy.

PRAYER

Lord, we need a great awakening. Let the holy fear of the Lord return to the church again. Father, cause this generation to return to Your ways. Let holiness and righteousness be honored in the church again. Let there be an increased awareness of Your presence, God, and a new hunger for righteousness. I desire to see Your glory cover the earth like the waters cover the sea. Let Your manifest presence return to the earth. Let revival break out in my country. Let the kingdom of God break in with power. Let miracles, signs, and wonders be released in my city.

I pray for our leaders: let them live lives of holiness and righteousness; let them be men and women of righteousness; let them carry the true burden of the Lord. Let the spirit of boldness come upon leaders to speak Your Word. I break the spirit of fear off of my leader. Let leaders be fearless and proclaim the gospel as they ought. I release boldness. I release revelation and insight from the Holy Ghost.

Let the power of the Holy Ghost empower leaders to preach with signs and wonders following. Let them be given utterances from heaven to make known the mysteries of the gospel. Let the leaders of this generation arise to be the ambassadors of Christ.

YOUR TURN

Use the space below to write out your own prayers and declarations.

_____

_____

_____

_____

_____

_____

_____

_____

_____

_____

_____

_____

_____

_____

_____

_____

RECEIVE INNER STRENGTH

SCRIPTURE

God is our refuge and strength, a well-proven help in trouble.

—Psalm 46:1

But those who wait upon the LORD shall renew their strength; they shall mount up with wings as eagles, they shall run and not be weary, and they shall walk and not faint.

—Isaiah 40:31

May He grant you out of the riches of His glory, to be strengthened and spiritually energized with power through His Spirit in your inner self [indwelling your innermost being and personality].

—Ephesians 3:16, AMP

I can do all things because of Christ who strengthens me.

—Philippians 4:13

DECLARATIONS

The Lord will cause me to awaken to my inner strength and arise to my full potential.

I petition God for strength and courage (Matt. 7:11).

The Lord will provide me with strength to persevere in the face of adversity.

In the presence of the Lord I find strength (Ps. 46:1). In the presence of the Lord there is peace, safety, and the fullness of joy.

Through Christ I can do all things, because He strengthens me (Phil. 4:13).

PRAYER

I am strong in the Lord and the power of His might. Father, strengthen me with might in my innermost being. Lord, You restore my soul daily. I ask, Lord, that You fill me with the knowledge of Your will in all wisdom and spiritual understanding that I might walk worthy of You and be fully pleasing to You. Strengthen me with all might according to Your glorious power. Give me patience and longsuffering with joyfulness. Lord, I want to be fruitful in every good work and increase in the knowledge of You.

YOUR TURN

Use the space below to write out your own prayers and declarations.

LIVE CONFIDENTLY

SCRIPTURE

Blessed is the man who trust in the LORD, and whose hope is the LORD.

—JEREMIAH 17:7

I can do all things because of Christ who strengthens me.

—PHILIPPIANS 4:13

Therefore do not throw away your confidence, which will be greatly rewarded.

—HEBREWS 10:35

This is the confidence that we have in Him, that if we ask anything according to His will, He hears us.

—1 JOHN 5:14

DECLARATIONS

I will move forward as the Lord leads even if I don't have all of the details figured out.

Confidence is a choice; I will seek biblical confidence today.

The Lord blesses those who find their confidence in Him (Jer. 17:7).

Biblical confidence will bring endurance, steadfastness, and consistency.

I will live out of a confidence based on my reliance on and trust in God.

Because of Christ, I can confidently approach God through faith (Eph. 3:12).

I will use my God-given gifts, and I will let my successes with those gifts boost my confidence.

Like Ruth and Naomi, I will be a woman of action.

I will confidently and decisively make decisions as the Lord places them in front of me.

I can approach God's throne with confidence (Heb. 4:16), and that will help me to live my life with confidence.

Confidence is about relying on God, so I will continue to trust Him.

It is better to trust in the Lord than to put confidence in man (Ps. 118:8).

It is better to trust in the Lord than to put confidence in princes (Ps. 118:9).

Lord, You are my confidence. You will keep my foot from being caught (Prov. 3:26).

I find refuge in the Lord, and in the fear of the Lord I find strong confidence (Prov. 14:26).

Father, I declare that You are the God of my salvation and the confidence of all the ends of the earth and far-off seas (Ps. 65:5).

PRAYER

Lord, You are my light and my salvation. I will not fear. I put my confidence in Your love for me. I am strong in the Lord and in the power of Your might. I will not be intimidated with mere men because I've encountered the true and living God. I will not throw away my confidence because it has great reward. My greatest desire is to be in Your will. My greatest confidence is found in Your will. You are the One who holds my life together.

YOUR TURN

Use the space below to write out your own prayers and declarations.

BECOME BOLD

SCRIPTURE

Have not I commanded you? Be strong and courageous. Do not be afraid or dismayed, for the LORD your God is with you wherever you go.

—JOSHUA 1:9

On the day I called, You answered me, and strengthened me in my soul.

—PSALM 138:3

The righteous are bold as a lion.

—PROVERBS 28:1

The Spirit of the Lord is upon Me, because He has anointed Me to preach the gospel to the poor; He has sent Me to heal the broken-hearted, to preach deliverance to the captives and recovery of sight to the blind, to set at liberty those who are oppressed; to preach the acceptable year of the Lord.

—LUKE 4:18–19

"Now, Lord, look on their threats and grant that Your servants may speak Your word with great boldness, by stretching out Your hand to heal and that signs and wonders may be performed in the name of Your holy Son Jesus." When they had prayed, the place where they were assembled together was shaken. And they were all filled with the Holy Spirit and spoke the word of God with boldness.

—Acts 4:29–31

Seeing then that we have such a hope, we speak with great boldness.

—2 Corinthians 3:12

Declarations

I will live with boldness and courage because the Lord is with me (Josh. 1:9).

Because of the hope of Christ, I will speak with boldness, declaring the gospel (2 Cor. 3:12).

I will stand for truth with boldness.

The Lord will grant me a holy boldness to speak His word (Acts 4:29).

Powers of darkness will be shattered when I speak prophetic declarations boldly.

I will stand boldly in the call of God.

I decree: Let there be great awakening to my soul. Let the fire of the Holy Ghost consume me. I embrace the boldness of the lioness.

Prayer

Now, Lord, look upon the threats of the enemy and grant to me the spirit of boldness that I may preach Your Word with miracles, signs, and wonders. Stretch

Your mighty hand over my life; empower me with right words at the right time. My confidence and trust is in You. Lord, give me courage to confront in love those who oppose Your Word.

I decree that I am a fearless and bold woman of God. I will answer the call to be an instrument of change in the earth. I will respond in crisis. I will boldly proclaim the gospel. In moral crisis I will boldly stand for truth. I will not be muzzled by the laws of the land. I will open my mouth wide, and You will fill it.

God, give me Your heart for my assignment. Give me Your perspective that I might be Your mouthpiece in the earth. I will stand up against injustice. I am the righteousness of God, and I am bold like a lion. I am fearless in the face of danger. I will preach the Word. I will go wherever You send me. In Jesus's name I pray. Amen.

YOUR TURN

Use the space below to write out your own prayers and declarations.

FIND YOUR GOD-GIVEN PURPOSE

SCRIPTURE

Do not think in your heart that you will escape in the king's palace any more than all the other Jews. For if you remain completely silent at this time, relief and deliverance will arise for the Jews from another place, but you and your father's house will perish. Yet who knows whether you have come to the kingdom for such a time as this?

—ESTHER 4:13–14, NKJV

If I perish, I perish.

—ESTHER 4:16

The LORD will fulfill His purpose for me; Your mercy, O LORD, endures forever; do not forsake the works of Your hands.

—PSALM 138:8

Now all has been heard. Let us hear the conclusion of the matter: Fear God and keep His commandments, for this is the whole duty of man.

—ECCLESIASTES 12:13

For I know the plans that I have for you, says the LORD, plans for peace and not for evil, to give you a future and a hope.

—JEREMIAH 29:11

Therefore, whether you eat, or drink, or whatever you do, do it all to the glory of God.

—1 Corinthians 10:31

For we are His workmanship, created in Christ Jesus for good works, which God prepared beforehand, so that we should walk in them.

—Ephesians 2:10

Declarations

God is awakening me to a purpose greater than myself. He is calling me from a mundane existence to a place of significance and fulfillment.

I will awaken from sleep and slumber.

I will awaken from complacency and indifference.

I am an active member in the army of the Lord.

I will engage the culture with my prayer and actions.

I loose confusion into every plan and demonic conspiracy to keep me silent.

I will arise and let my voice be heard.

I will preach Your Word.

I will encourage the next generation of godly women.

Let every dormant gift, talent, and anointing be awakened inside of me.

Let every God-given idea be awakened, activated, cultivated, and implemented for kingdom advancement.

I will answer the call of God.

I will not cower in fear.

I loose myself from insecurity and fear of failure.

I break every religious spirit that has pushed me to the background.

I shake myself free from apathy and a lack of concern.

I will redeem the time in my life.

I will not allow a lazy, slothful spirit to control my life.

I will walk circumspectly, not as a foolish, silly, gullible woman. I am wise and know what the will of the Lord is for my life.

The Lord will redeem all lost time and restore every wasted year.

I will capitalize on every appropriate opportunity to fulfill my destiny.

I am a woman filled with the Holy Spirit.

My heart is experiencing a great awakening to my purpose and destiny.

I will seek and find the God who calls me.

I have vision and insight into the heart and mind of God.

There is a new level of urgency and passion for purpose arising in my heart.

I am significant.

I loose myself from hopelessness and despondency.

The Lord validates me, and He has called me and anointed me for such a time as this.

I will use my life and resources to accomplish great things for the Lord.

I am not in this world by chance; God has a vision for my future.

God has ordained me to be a woman filled with His purpose.

I am the outcome of something God envisioned.

When others try to discredit and devalue me, I will draw from the Lord and seek only to obey His commands.

I will seek the vision of the Lord and with it find clarity, inspiration, structure, and motivation.

PRAYERS

Lord, Your Word says in Deuteronomy 30:19, "I call heaven and earth as witnesses today against you, that I have set before you life and death, blessing and cursing; therefore choose life, that both you and your descendants may live" (NKJV).

Lord, I choose life. I choose blessings. I ask that You would give me the ability to make sound decisions. Let wisdom and discretion rest upon me. I choose to follow Your plans and purpose for my life. I choose to step out of my comfort zone and obey Your will for my life.

I will not be a victim of circumstance. I choose to forgive every man who has withheld promotions from me because I am a woman. I will not let a spirit of hatred of men infiltrate my heart. I will not let revenge, anger, and retaliation contaminate my spirit.

I will make godly choices motivated by love. I will walk in righteousness. I choose to be a woman of holiness. I choose to break out of the status quo. I choose to be a blessing to the next generation. I will leave a legacy of goodness and mercy in the earth. I draw a line in the spirit and choose life that my bloodline will be blessed. Because of my righteous choice, my descendants will inherit the earth. In Jesus's name I pray. Amen.

I thank You, my Lord, that I am Your workmanship. You are the Potter, and I am the clay uniquely designed to bring You glory. I ask, dear God, that You will awaken vision inside me. I don't want to waste my life doing things You didn't design me to do. I have a responsibility to You, my Creator, to use my life for Your plans and purpose. So I ask, dear God, that You would cause me to perceive Your heart and mind for me. Lead me and guide me that I might be all You designed me to be. Order my steps; show me the way I should go. Help me to set goals that are realistic and aligned with Your purposes. In Jesus's name I pray. Amen.

Lord, Your Word says that faith without works is dead. I break all spirits of procrastination in my life. I will write the vision for my life. I will not hesitate and procrastinate any longer. Your Word says that without a vision Your people perish. I declare that I am a woman of vision. I have a unique purpose to fulfill in the earth. I will not let the devil steal my time and days. I break all spirits of slothfulness and apathy in the name of Jesus. Amen.

YOUR TURN

Use the space below to write out your own prayers and declarations.

_____

_____

_____

_____

_____

_____

_____

_____

_____

SEE YOURSELF AS GOD SEES YOU

SCRIPTURES

God saw everything that He had made, and indeed it was very good.

—GENESIS 1:31

You made all the delicate, inner parts of my body and knit me together in my mother's womb. Thank you for making me so wonderfully complex! Your workmanship is marvelous—how well I know it!

—PSALM 139:13–14, NLT

For the LORD takes pleasure in His people; He will beautify the meek with salvation.

—PSALM 149:4

As the bridegroom rejoices over the bride, so your God shall rejoice over you.

—ISAIAH 62:5

The LORD your God is in your midst, a Mighty One, who will save. He will rejoice over you with gladness, He will renew you with His love, He will rejoice over you with singing.

—ZEPHANIAH 3:17

For it is God who works in you both to will and to do for His good pleasure.

—PHILIPPIANS 2:13, NKJV

Declarations

I choose to meditate on the things that are true.

I loose myself from all falsehood.

I believe the truth of God's Word concerning who I am.

Through the power of God, I uproot every lie and deception planted in my mind.

The Lord's thoughts about me are precious (Ps. 139:17).

The Lord rejoices over me (Isa. 62:5; Zeph. 3:17).

I am fearfully and wonderfully made (Ps. 139:14).

Prayers

Lord, let the truth of Your Word arise in my heart.

"How precious also are Your thoughts to me, O God! How great is the sum of them!" (Ps. 139:17). Lord, I believe Your thoughts toward me are great. I am always on Your mind. I believe that Your thoughts toward me are good and not evil.

As Isaiah 62:5 says, I believe You rejoice over me as Your creation. I am made in Your image. I bring You glory when I do Your will in the earth.

Lord, I have felt like You've forgotten or rejected me as a woman. I believe You love me, and I receive Your love. I loose myself from father rejection. I am not forgotten, cast aside, or thrown away. I receive the spirit of adoption, and I cry, "Abba, Father." I repent of these thoughts. I believe my name is written on the palm of Your hand.

Lord, open my spiritual ears to hear the songs You are singing over me (Zeph. 3:17). *I choose to rest in Your love. I will no longer strive to be accepted. Don't stop filling me with Your love.*

Father, I ask that You give me Your heart for my life. Enlighten the eyes of my understanding. Help me to know why You created me. What did we talk about before I was in my mother's womb? What were You thinking when You knit me in my mother's womb? Fill my heart and my mind with Your thoughts toward me.

Lord, I desire to do everything You purposed me to do. Give me grace to fulfill Your call on my life. Lord, I need a holy visitation. Pour out the Spirit of knowledge upon my life. I want a living understanding of who I am before Your throne. Cause me to see life from Your perspective.

Your Turn

Use the space below to write out your own prayers and declarations.

_____

_____

_____

BE DELIVERED FROM THE ORPHAN SPIRIT

SCRIPTURE

Yet to all who received Him, He gave the power to become sons of God, to those who believed in His name, who were born not of blood, nor of the will of the flesh, nor of the will of man, but of God.

—JOHN 1:12–13

For you have not received the spirit of slavery again to fear. But you have received the Spirit of adoption, by whom we cry, "Abba, Father."

—ROMANS 8:15

You are all sons of God by faith in Christ Jesus.

—GALATIANS 3:26

Consider how much love the Father has given to us, that we should be called children of God. Therefore the world does not know us, because it did not know Him.

—1 JOHN 3:1

DECLARATIONS

In the presence of the Lord I will find confidence to fulfill the mission of the Lord.

I will pray and fast until I find myself at home in the arms of the Father.

The love the Father has for me is bigger than my rejection and fear.

I will call out, "Abba, Father," to the Lord.

I am a child of God.

The Lord has adopted me as His daughter.

PRAYER

Lord, I thank You that You love me. I receive Your love. Let the power of Your blood cleanse me from the orphan spirit. Baptize my heart with the fire of Your love. Let the fire of Your love burn away the rejection and fear. Let the fire of Your love purge away the dross of the orphan spirit. Your love is like vehement flames, and many waters cannot quench Your love for me. The flames of Your love for me are eternal, and many floods will never be able to drown it out. Your Word says that You will not leave us as orphans but You will come to us.

Holy Spirit, come and pour the love of God into my heart. Holy Spirit, teach me how to receive the love of the Father. Come empower me with the truth of Your love. I loose myself from the survivalist mentality. I don't want to just survive; I want to enjoy the abundant life You have for me. I am tired of making fig leaves for myself. I am tired of living in fear and shame. I will no longer hide from Your presence.

I humble myself, Lord. Your Word says that unless a kernel of wheat falls to the ground and dies, it will not bear fruit. I choose to die to self. I will not only be concerned with my best interest, but I will also use my authority to benefit the well-being of others. I shake myself free from passivity and indifference.

I am a daughter of the King. I am not an orphan. I don't have to perform to receive Your love. I receive the spirit of adoption, and I cry, "Abba, Father." I loose myself from all insecurity and fear. I loose myself from self-preservation.

Forgive me for being obsessed with trying to keep things I've obtained through striving and competing. No longer will I compete to survive. I have favor with You. I trust Your love to protect me. I find my security in You. You are my heavenly Father; You provide for me. I choose to obey Your Word. I will no longer try to save my life, but I choose to lose it in the arms of Your love. Amen.

YOUR TURN

Use the space below to write out your own prayers and declarations.

LET GO OF BITTERNESS

SCRIPTURE

Create in me a clean heart, O God, and renew a right spirit within me.

—PSALM 51:10

Let all bitterness, wrath, anger, outbursts, and blasphemies, with all malice, be taken away from you. And be kind one to another, tenderhearted, forgiving one another, just as God in Christ also forgave you.

—EPHESIANS 4:31–32

Exercise foresight and be on the watch to look [after one another], to see that no one falls back from and fails to secure God's grace (His unmerited favor and spiritual blessing), in order that no root of resentment (rancor, bitterness, or hatred) shoots forth and causes trouble and bitter torment, and the many become contaminated and defiled by it.

—HEBREWS 12:15, AMPC

Therefore, my beloved brothers, let every man be swift to hear, slow to speak, and slow to anger, for the anger of man does not work the righteousness of God.

—JAMES 1:19–20

But if you have bitter envying and strife in your hearts, do not boast and do not lie against the truth.

—JAMES 3:14

DECLARATIONS

I will turn to Christ for help when I am bitter.

I will allow all bitterness to be removed from my life (Eph. 4:31).

I will replace bitterness with love (1 Cor. 13:4–7).

I will remove bitterness before it can destroy my peace.

I will let go of bitterness, leaving it to God to handle.

I will be slow to anger (James 1:19–20).

Bitterness, hurt, and unforgiveness will not rule my life.

I will confess my bitterness and disappointment to God and know that He is working out even those for my good.

PRAYER

Lord, remove all mixture of the negative life experience from my behavior and values. I choose to be better and not bitter. Let the fire of the Holy Ghost purge away bitterness, anger, frustration, and disappointment.

Lord, I ask that You create in me a clean heart and renew a righteous spirit within me. I repent of all bitterness, anger, and desire for revenge. I forgive those who have caused me pain. I forgive those who have disappointed me. I release You, Lord, from anything that

I think You owe me because I may have felt let down or did not understand Your timing. I know that You are faithful, that You never fail, and that You are always with me. I repent for blaming You for things I invited into my life because of disobedience, ignorance, or rebellion. I repent for blaming you for the things the enemy has done to sabotage Your perfect will for my life.

Right now, in the name of Jesus, I loose myself from all spirits of retaliation. I loose myself from all critical and cynical spirits that have entered my life through bitterness. I will no longer drink from bitter waters, but I will trust in the Tree of Life to turn my sorrow into joy. I choose to love and believe in the goodness of the Lord that brings repentance.

Lord, remove the bitter taste of hurt, pain, loss, and rejection from my life. I choose to taste and see that You are good. Let Your goodness fill my life. In Jesus's name, amen.

YOUR TURN

Use the space below to write out your own prayers and declarations.

PULL DOWN STRONGHOLDS

SCRIPTURE

No temptation has taken you except what is common to man. God is faithful, and He will not permit you to be tempted above what you can endure, but will with the temptation also make a way to escape, that you may be able to bear it.

—1 CORINTHIANS 10:13

For though we walk in the flesh, we do not war according to the flesh. For the weapons of our warfare are not carnal, but mighty through God to the pulling down of strongholds, casting down imaginations and every high thing that exalts itself against the knowledge of God, bringing every thought into captivity to the obedience of Christ.

—2 CORINTHIANS 10:3–5

For our fight is not against flesh and blood, but against principalities, against powers, against the rulers of the darkness of this world, and against spiritual forces of evil in the heavenly places.

—EPHESIANS 6:12

DECLARATIONS

By the power of almighty God, I demolish every stronghold opposing the will of God for my life!

The Lord will provide me with weapons of spiritual warfare that will pull down strongholds (2 Cor. 10:3–5).

I can break through every obstacle by embracing the power and ability Jesus provides.

PRAYER

Lord, I know that my warfare is not against flesh and blood, so I am not angry or upset with men. I know my enemy has been the devil. I will not resort to carnal, weak weapons of hatred and retaliation. I choose weapons that are mighty and empowered by You to pull down strongholds. I choose to apply the Word of God. I plead the blood of Jesus to my mind. I use the name of Jesus to demolish strongholds set up in my mind by erroneous teaching. I bind every arrogant and rebellious idea in my mind. I cast down lofty imaginations and pride in my mind. I submit my thought life to the words of Christ, "Blessed are the pure in heart, for they shall see God" (Matt. 5:8). In Jesus's name, amen.

YOUR TURN

Use the space below to write out your own prayers and declarations.

FIGHT FEAR

SCRIPTURE

Be strong and of a good courage. Fear not, nor be afraid of them, for the LORD your God, it is He who goes with you. He will not fail you, nor forsake you.

—DEUTERONOMY 31:6

Even though I walk through the valley of the shadow of death, I will fear no evil; for You are with me; Your rod and Your staff, they comfort me.

—PSALM 23:4

Who is the [woman] who fears the LORD? He will teach [her] in the way He should choose. [She] will dwell at ease, and [her] descendants will inherit the land. The counsel of the LORD is with those who fear him, and He will make His covenant known to them. My eyes are ever toward the LORD, for He will lead my feet from the net.

—PSALM 25:12–15

I sought the LORD, and He answered me, and delivered me from all my fears.

—PSALM 34:4

In the day when I am afraid, I will trust in You.

—PSALM 56:3

Peace I leave with you. My peace I give to you. Not as the world gives do I give to you. Let not your heart be troubled, neither let it be afraid.

—JOHN 14:27

For God has not given us the spirit of fear, but of power, and love, and self-control.

—2 TIMOTHY 1:7

There is no fear in love, but perfect love casts out fear, because fear has to do with punishment. Whoever fears is not perfect in love.

—1 JOHN 4:18

DECLARATIONS

I do not have to live in fear; instead I can live in the presence of the Lord, which casts out fear.

I will trust in the Lord when I am afraid (Ps. 56:3).

The Lord is with me when I am afraid.

I was not made to live in fear; I was made to have a spirit of power and love and self-control (2 Tim. 1:7).

The Lord's perfect love will cast out all fear in me (1 John 4:18).

God is moving me from inferiority, competition, and fear to power, influence, and courage.

I declare that I will arise from fear and embrace the courage of the Lord.

I will not cower in fear.

I am fearless and fierce. I will walk in the fullness of my call, I will chase my dreams, and I will seek out opportunities to be light in a dark world.

PRAYER

Lord, I will be strong and very courageous. Your perfect love casts out fear. Draw me by Your Spirit into the secret chambers of Your love. Lord, You are my refuge and my fortress. My God, in You do I trust. I will be anxious for nothing, but in everything by prayer and supplication with thanksgiving, I will make my requests known unto You. I set my affections and love upon You. I draw nigh to You, and You draw nigh to me.

I trust You with my whole heart, leaning not on my understanding. I search for Your wisdom. I cast all my cares upon You, for You care for me. Lord, You are my strong fortress; I run to You, and I am safe. Amen.

YOUR TURN

Use the space below to write out your own prayers and declarations.

TRIUMPH OVER TRAUMA

SCRIPTURE

God is our refuge and strength, a well-proven help in trouble.

—PSALM 46:1

To all who mourn in Israel, he will give a crown of beauty for ashes, a joyous blessing instead of mourning, festive praise instead of despair. In their righteousness, they will be like great oaks that the LORD has planted for his own glory.

—ISAIAH 61:3, NLT

Not only so, but we also boast in tribulation, knowing that tribulation produces patience, patience produces character, and character produces hope. And hope does not disappoint, because the love of God is shed abroad in our hearts by the Holy Spirit who has been given to us.

—ROMANS 5:3–5

I can do all things because of Christ who strengthens me.

—PHILIPPIANS 4:13

My brothers, count it all joy when you fall into diverse temptations, knowing that the trying of your faith develops patience. But let patience perfect its work, that you may be perfect and complete, lacking nothing.

—JAMES 1:2–4

God blesses those who patiently endure testing and temptation. Afterward they will receive the crown of life that God has promised to those who love him.

—JAMES 1:12, NLT

DECLARATIONS

The Lord will give me beauty from my ashes.

God is my healer; with Him I will triumph over adversity and grow through it (Rom. 5:3–5).

This is my moment to be healed and set free.

I declare that my light has come. No longer will I sit in darkness, for the Lord is releasing heavenly revelation and illumination to me. My purpose is getting clearer.

I am a woman who has mental, emotional, and spiritual fortitude. New strength is arising within me.

I choose to move forward in the face of trauma. I will sustain a sense of personal meaning in life. I will not be destroyed by the events that happen to me. I receive inner strength to overcome.

I declare that I will not let difficult or traumatic events define and derail my destiny. I will not allow a spirit of bitterness, hurt, and unforgiveness to rule my life. I refuse to have a victim's mentality.

I am strong and able to withstand opposition. I will continue blessing and serving the Lord and others even in the midst of storms and crises (Phil. 4:13).

I am the arrow of deliverance that the Lord is polishing to strategically shoot out from His quiver.

I am a woman who is able to bear up under pressure and adversity.

I am conspicuous, distinguished, outstanding, and pre-eminent. I will shine bright like a diamond for the King of glory.

PRAYER

Lord, You are my refuge and my strength, my very present help in times of adversity. I embrace Your healing and deliverance. You are my glory and the lifter of my head. The brightness of God's countenance is turned toward me. I am the apple of Your eye, and the favor and glory of the Lord will arise over me. Lord, clothe me in a mantle of dignity and strength. In Jesus's name I pray. Amen.

YOUR TURN

Use the space below to write out your own prayers and declarations.

Part III

OUTER TRANSFORMATION

G OD IS RELEASING His power through women so they will make the lives of those in their spheres of influence utterly different than they were before. Many will challenge your authority to preach or teach the gospel. They will use every scripture out of context to silence your voice, but there will be one undeniable, unstoppable, unkillable force moving through you that will silence all the gainsayers: the power of God.

The limitless displays of the power of God will gain the attention of kings and presidents. Miracles will open doors of opportunities to preach the gospel in unusual places. The Holy Spirit will give you power to change, transform, or affect people, places, and events. You will see this power at work in you so mightily that just your presence will cause things to change without your needing to directly force them to happen. This is the influence the Holy Spirit will grant you as you allow Him to fill you.

The Lord wants to reach people of all nations and bring them to salvation—and He wants to use you to do it. He is already using women who will operate in resurrection power to deliver those who are oppressed, bring healing, and preach the gospel to the lost. The prayers and declarations in this section will empower you to walk in the fullness of God's call for you. There are no limits to what God can do through you except the ones you impose on yourself. Let the Lord empower you with miraculous power to influence human hearts for the glory of God.

DISCOVER GOD'S CALL

SCRIPTURE

There are many plans in a man's heart, nevertheless the counsel of the LORD will stand.

—PROVERBS 19:21

You did not choose Me, but I chose you, and appointed you, that you should go and bear fruit, and that your fruit should remain, that the Father may give you whatever you ask Him in My name.

—JOHN 15:16

We have diverse gifts according to the grace that is given to us: if prophecy, according to the proportion of faith; if service, in serving; he who teaches, in teaching; he who exhorts, in exhortation; he who gives, with generosity; he who rules, with diligence; he who shows mercy, with cheerfulness.

—ROMANS 12:6–8

For to this you were called, because Christ suffered for us, leaving us an example, that you should follow His steps: "He committed no sin, nor was deceit found in His mouth." When He was reviled, He did not revile back; when He suffered, He did not threaten, but He entrusted Himself to Him who judges righteously.

—1 PETER 2:21–23

As everyone has received a gift, even so serve one another with it, as good stewards of the manifold grace of God.

—1 PETER 4:10

DECLARATIONS

I will seek the Lord and His plan for my life, for His plan is better than my own.

I will use the giftings and talents the Lord has given me for His glory.

The Lord chose and appointed me to bear His fruit (John 15:16).

I will steward the gifts God has given me (1 Pet. 4:10).

PRAYERS

Lord, I pray that You will show me my place in the church. Let me discover my unique talents and gifts that I may arise and become active in building Your church and advancing Your purposes in the earth. Let me be a woman of courage and boldness who speaks Your truth in love. Let me disciple and train the next generation of godly women. Let me be intentional about reproducing a generation of women who are feminine and powerful.

Let me be a woman of grace and dignity. Let me model a woman who is constant and steadfast in the work of the kingdom.

Father, help me develop sound wisdom and judgment in everything I do. Increase my influence; let my voice be heard in this hour.

Father, I thank You that my times are in Your hands. You make all things new. I thank You, Lord, that You take the ashes of my life and make them beautiful. Lord, let this be a season of the great exchange. Let the oil of joy be poured into my life for the spirit of mourning. I will no longer mourn what I have lost. Lord, I ask that You will cause my joy to be full. I decree that the joy of the Lord is my strength. I will not wallow in self-pity. I break off the spirits of heaviness, depression, and oppression. I wrap myself in the garment of praise. Instead of the shame of a widow or barren woman, I will have double honor. Instead of confusion, I will walk in revelation and understanding. I shall rejoice in my portion. Just as Ruth did, I will pioneer a new path of glory and double honor. I trust You, Lord, and where You lead I will follow. In Jesus's name, amen.

Where Your Spirit leads me, I will follow. I humble myself under Your mighty hand. Lord, You said in Your Word that obedience is better than sacrifice. I will obey Your leadings. I will walk in Your ways. I

will trust You with my whole heart, leaning not on my own understanding, and You will exalt me in due season. Amen.

Father, I pray that You will open my eyes to the new things You are doing in my life. I declare that I will embrace new possibilities. Your plan for me is good and not evil. Your plan is to give me a hope and a future. Lord, I believe You speak from my future and that everything in my life is already finished in You. I will arise in faith and depend on You to show me the path of life. What is my path? Lord, I ask that You reveal it to me by Your Spirit.

Father, bring divine connections into my life. Connect me with mentors and coaches who will help me fulfill my destiny. Lord, I ask that You deliver me from dream thieves. Holy Spirit, awaken the dream of the Lord in my life. Make me a blessing to my generation. Let me bring favor to someone else.

YOUR TURN

Use the space below to write out your own prayers and declarations.

BREAK BARRIERS

SCRIPTURE

For though we walk in the flesh, we do not war according to the flesh. For the weapons of our warfare are not carnal, but mighty through God to the pulling down of strongholds.

—2 CORINTHIANS 10:3–4

Therefore you are no longer a slave (bond-servant), but a son; and if a son, then also an heir through [the gracious act of] God [through Christ].

—GALATIANS 4:7, AMP

For He is our peace, who has made both groups one and has broken down the barrier of the dividing wall.

—EPHESIANS 2:14

But we are not of those who draw back to destruction, but of those who have faith to the saving of the soul.

—HEBREWS 10:39

DECLARATIONS

I will step over every barrier to achieve what God has called me to do.

Jesus Christ Himself broke down barriers and unified the church (Eph. 2:14); through Him, I will fight to do the same.

Decisiveness and resolution will be the beginning of my breakthrough.

With the Lord's help, I will make difficult and risky decisions with expedience to break the barriers I face.

I will stand strong in my decisions.

God has provided me with all I need to succeed and break down barriers; I will have confidence in that fact.

Through my faith, I will break barriers.

I will petition the Lord in faith and follow Him to move beyond obstacles I face.

I will not draw back; I will lean in, step up, and refuse to turn back (Heb. 10:39).

With God, all things are possible (Matt. 19:26).

When I pray in faith, barriers will be broken.

I will not sit idly and wait for barriers to fall down around me; I will take an active role.

Declarations for breaking national, ethnic, and racial barriers

Through the Lord, ethnic and racial boundaries can be removed.

I can remove and will remove animosity and judgment toward people different from me, no matter how many years it has been building up (Ruth 1:16–17).

I will be diligent, faithful, and kind, and I will pray the Lord uses that to break down barriers around me.

I honor the cultural differences between me and those around me. I seek to understand and appreciate the racial differences. I will not discriminate. I will not prejudge. I will overcome hate with love. Lord, I repent for being a respecter of persons. Lord, I give You permission to search my heart and lead me into truth. If I've walked in racial prejudice, I repent. I ask, Father, that You would burn Your love in my heart for all mankind.

I will stand out from people around me because of my gifts.

Declarations for breaking religious barriers

If people question my faith in the living God, I will let my actions speak for me.

The body of Christ sometimes seems varied, but it is one group, under Christ (John 10:16).

In Christ, we are all one (Col. 3:11).

In the Great Commission, Jesus sent us to tell the good news to all people in all cultures; our cultural differences don't mean we have to stay divided.

The Father will unite His church.

Declarations for breaking family and generational boundaries

With the Lord, the power of generational curses can be broken.

I resolve to live a different life than that of my family.

I will remove myself from the broken family of my past and cleave to the new family the Lord gives me (Ruth 1:16–17).

I will not allow a family or generational curse to hold me back from the will of God for my life.

Declarations for breaking class and economic barriers

God is raising up people who will break the barrier of poverty!

With God and through diligence, faith, and determination, I can overcome poverty.

I will work hard to overcome this barrier rather than waiting for someone to help me.

I will not work selfishly for my own gain; I will work for the benefit of my loved ones.

Declarations for breaking gender barriers

My God-given confidence will help me break gender barriers.

I will refuse to believe stereotypes about women, and thus I remove their power over my life.

I will not even entertain the lowly, limited choices society deems are acceptable to me; instead, I will listen for the voice of the Lord and follow His plan for my life.

I am a woman, and I refuse to allow that fact to keep me from doing what must be done to care for myself and those I love.

Even in a male-dominated society, God will restore and redeem the lives of women; God will restore and redeem me.

My kindness and strong work ethic will allow me to break barriers.

PRAYER

I decree that this is my season of breakthrough. I decree that every limitation and barrier obstructing my destiny is broken. I will not be defined by my economic status. I will not be limited by my gender or race. I decree that every ceiling is broken. I am a woman who will expand and break out on the left and the right. I will accomplish everything the Lord has designed for my life. I will rise up and stand up in the anointing. I speak to every mountain of fear and command you to be moved and cast into the sea. I will arise above prejudice and every preconceived opinion about my abilities as a woman. I break every generational curse of poverty and lack. I press on toward the high calling in Christ Jesus. I am a trailblazer. I will finish strong. I will come through!

YOUR TURN

Use the space below to write out your own prayers and declarations.

_____

_____

_____

_____

_____

_____

_____

_____

_____

_____

_____

_____

_____

_____

_____

_____

_____

TAKE ACTION

Scripture

Not everyone who says to Me, "Lord, Lord," shall enter the kingdom of heaven, but he who does the will of My Father who is in heaven.

—Matthew 7:21

For I have given you an example, that you should do as I have done to you. Truly, truly I say to you, a servant is not greater than his master, nor is he who is sent greater than he who sent him. If you know these things, blessed are you if you do them.

—John 13:15–17

Be doers of the word and not hearers only, deceiving yourselves. For if anyone is a hearer of the word and not a doer, he is like a man viewing his natural face in a mirror. He views himself, and goes his way, and immediately forgets what kind of man he was. But whoever looks into the perfect law of liberty, and continues in it, and is not a forgetful hearer but a doer of the work, this man will be blessed in his deeds.

—James 1:22–25

Religion that is pure and undefiled before God, the Father, is this: to visit the fatherless and widows in their affliction and to keep oneself unstained by the world.

—James 1:27

What does it profit, my brothers, if a man says he has faith but has no works? Can faith save him? If a brother or sister is naked and lacking daily food, and one of you says to them, "Depart in peace, be warmed and filled," and yet you give them nothing that the body needs, what does it profit? So faith by itself, if it has no works, is dead.

—James 2:14–17

DECLARATIONS

I decree I am a go-getter.

I will not delay in keeping the commandments of the Lord (Ps. 119:60).

I will not draw back from the challenges of life.

I will be a doer of the Word rather than just a hearer (James 1:22).

I will work as unto the Lord (Col. 3:23–24).

I will live my destiny; I will live a passion-filled life.

God is interested in promoting women who are fruitful, those who are ready to do something. I will be the woman ready to take action.

PRAYER

I will arise to fulfill my destiny. Lord, where You lead I will follow. Take me to the mountain of change. Let me be transformed by touching Your glory. Awaken passion in my heart. I choose to love fearlessly. I believe I am chosen to bear fruit in my life. Father, release boldness in my life to break every barrier set up by the devil to stop me from pleasing You. I will be a living epistle read by men.

YOUR TURN

Use the space below to write out your own prayers and declarations.

WIN THE LOST

SCRIPTURE

Also I heard the voice of the Lord saying, "Whom shall I send, and who will go for us?" Then I said, "Here am I. Send me."

—ISAIAH 6:8

Then He said to His disciples, "The harvest truly is plentiful, but the laborers are few."

—MATTHEW 9:37

Go therefore and make disciples of all nations, baptizing them in the name of the Father and of the Son and of the Holy Spirit, teaching them to observe all things I have commanded you.

—MATTHEW 28:19–20

But you shall receive power when the Holy Spirit comes upon you. And you shall be My witnesses in Jerusalem, and in all Judea and Samaria, and to the ends of the earth.

—ACTS 1:8

DECLARATIONS

I will do my part to win the lost; I will answer the call of the Great Commission.

I will honor the Lord and spread His Word by committing myself to evangelism even when it is difficult.

Here am I, Lord. Send me (Isa. 6:8).

I will be a laborer to bring in the harvest (Matt. 9:37).

Prayer

Lord of the harvest, we pray that You would send forth laborers into the fields. Give believers Your heart for souls. I pray that honor for the evangelist would return to the church. Lord, we repent for not winning souls. Your Word says he who wins souls is wise (Prov. 11:30). Let the spirit of hardness of heart be broken off of believers. Let the scales be removed from our eyes to see the harvest all around us. Let fear and intimidation be broken off of believers. Let us trust You to give us words to speak. Lead us to those to whom we are called to minister the gospel of salvation. Order our steps in Your Word. Let the preachers and proclaimers return to the church.

Your Turn

Use the space below to write out your own prayers and declarations.

SEEK UNITY

Scripture

How good and how pleasant it is for brothers to dwell together in unity! It is like precious oil upon the head, that runs down on the beard—even Aaron's beard.

—Psalm 133:1–2

Two are better than one, because they have a good [more satisfying] reward for their labor; for if they fall, the one will lift up his fellow. But woe to him who is alone when he falls and has not another to lift him up! Again, if two lie down together, then they have warmth; but how can one be warm alone? And though a man might prevail against him who is alone, two will withstand him. A threefold cord is not quickly broken.

—Ecclesiastes 4:9–12, ampc

Again I say to you, that if two of you agree on earth about anything they ask, it will be done for them by My Father who is in heaven.

—Matthew 18:19

For by one Spirit we are all baptized into one body, whether we are Jews or Gentiles, whether we are slaves or free, and we have all been made to drink of one Spirit. The body is not one part, but many.

—1 Corinthians 12:13–14

Only let your conduct be worthy of the gospel of Christ, that whether or not I come and see you, I may hear of your activities, that you are standing fast in one spirit, with one mind, striving together for the faith of the gospel.

—PHILIPPIANS 1:27

DECLARATIONS

With Christ at the center of our relationships, separation and division among the church will disappear.

The church is one body; members may have different functions, but I will remember we all must work together to bring God the glory.

I am one part of the body of Christ; I will work in conjunction with others.

I will seek and encourage unity within the church.

PRAYERS

Lord, Your Word says how good and pleasant it is for the brethren to dwell together in unity. I pray that You will pour out the bonding oil of unity. Make us one. Let the church experience Your commanded blessing, life forevermore. Break down the wall of separation and division. Let those who spread seeds of discord among the brethren be convicted. Lord, I pray that You will heal Your sons and daughters and make us one. I pray that You will make us one as You and Jesus are one.

Let loving each other be our highest goal in ministry. Let us learn to love one another that the world may know You came. Let the spirit of love became so tangible that men can see and feel it in the great congregation. Let us fall in love with You so that we may love one another.

I bind all spirits of competition. I loose unity and cooperation. I bind cruelty and jealousy. I bind the spirit of pride and fear. I loose humility and love.

Father, we understand that we cannot love in our own strength. Holy Spirit, empower us to love one another. Pour out the love of God in our hearts.

Lord, I thank You for the new thing You're doing in the body of Christ. I thank You for the unity and collaboration between men and women in ministry. Lord, I ask that You will cause the body of Christ to think outside the box of religion and tradition. I declare that walls of separation and division will crumble and fall. I bind every evil work of division and competition between men and women. I ask that You will pour out the bonding oil of unity (Ps. 133). *Let a new level of respect and honor arise between men and women. Let our conduct be worthy of the gospel. Let men and women stand together in one spirit and with one mind striving together for the sake of the gospel* (Phil. 1:27). *Let us put aside our petty differences and humble*

ourselves under Your mighty hand. Lord, I pray that the body of Christ will move together in one accord. Let us be like-minded and walk in love (Phil. 2:2). I repent for our selfish ambitions and conceit. Lord, I pray that You will make us one as You and the Father are one (John 17). Let us esteem one another better than ourselves. Let us identify each gift and not over-step our measure of rule. Let each person align in his or her proper rank and column as the army of the Lord. Let us collaborate and create to advance the kingdom of God in our spheres of influence.

I command every wall of division and suspicion to fall between men and women in leadership. There is safety in numbers. I will not be a woman who is isolated and outside the protection of a team. I choose to trust those in leadership over me. I am not God's alternative plan. I am specifically and intentionally called, anointed, and appointed to fulfill His kingdom purposes in the earth. In Jesus's name, amen.

YOUR TURN

Use the space below to write out your own prayers and declarations.

BECOME A GREAT LEADER

SCRIPTURE

But Jesus called them together, and said, "You know that those who are appointed to rule over the Gentiles lord it over them, and their great ones exercise authority over them. But it shall not be so among you. Whoever would be great among you must be your servant, and whoever among you would be greatest must be servant of all. For even the Son of Man came not to be served, but to serve, and to give His life as a ransom for many."

—MARK 10:42–45

Let nothing be done out of strife or conceit, but in humility let each esteem the other better than himself. Let each of you look not only to your own interests, but also to the interests of others.

—PHILIPPIANS 2:3–4

As everyone has received a gift, even so serve one another with it, as good stewards of the manifold grace of God.

—1 PETER 4:10

DECLARATIONS

I was created to express God's rule and reign.

God created me with the gift of leadership to influence and impact the world.

As a servant-leader, I will seek to serve God's people rather than be served by them.

God raised me up and set me in a position of leadership.

I will allow the Holy Spirit to shape me into a leader.

As a leader, I will seek to serve God's people, not to be served.

PRAYER

Lord, I ask that You will awaken the gift of leadership inside me. I desire to lead Your people with all diligence, righteousness, and integrity. Let me be a leader who represents You and Your character. Let me be a leader who speaks the truth in love, meeting the needs of Your people (Rom. 12:8).

Let my life reflect the holy standard of the kingdom. Give me the grace to stand in front of Your people, leading them with Your heart and mind.

Let Your anointing and grace rest on me to speak words of encouragement, correction, direction, vision, and purpose. Give me eyes to see the potential You've placed inside Your people. Give me wisdom to direct them to path of righteousness. Give me insight to instruct and train them to be mighty warriors with hearts to serve Your purposes.

YOUR TURN

Use the space below to write out your own prayers and declarations.

_____

_____

_____

_____

_____

_____

_____

_____

_____

_____

_____

_____

_____

_____

_____

_____

_____

SPEAK WISE WORDS

SCRIPTURE

Honest words never hurt anyone, but what's the point of all this pious bluster?
—JOB 6:25, THE MESSAGE

How sweet are Your words to the taste of my mouth! Sweeter than honey to my mouth!
—PSALM 119:103

Death and life are in the power of the tongue.
—PROVERBS 18:21

Let no unwholesome word proceed out of your mouth, but only that which is good for building up, that it may give grace to the listeners.
—EPHESIANS 4:29

Let your speech always be with grace, seasoned with salt, that you may know how you should answer everyone.
—COLOSSIANS 4:6

DECLARATIONS

My mouth is a well of life, and its words bring healing and wholeness to the wounded (Prov. 10:11).

I decree that wisdom is found on my lips and I am a woman of understanding (Prov. 10:13).

I will speak words that edify, exhort, and comfort those in my sphere of influence (1 Cor. 14:3).

My tongue will be like the pen of the ready writer, writing the plans and purpose of God on the hearts of those I influence (Ps. 45:1).

I will be a woman who restrains my lips and demonstrates wisdom (Prov. 10:19).

My lips will feed many with truth and insight (Prov. 10:21).

PRAYER

Lord, Your Word states that right words are forcible. Let me speak words that are appropriate for every occasion. Teach me, Lord, to hold my tongue. Cause me to know where I have erred. I repent for injustice in my tongue (Job 6:24–25, 30). *Lord, show me the places where my words have caused confusion, strife, and division. I ask that You will put Your sweet words in my mouth that I may bring peace and encouragement to those in my sphere of influence. Let the words of my mouth and the meditations of my heart be pure and acceptable before You* (Ps. 19:14). *I pray that You will create in me a clean heart and renew a righteous spirit within me* (Ps. 51:10). *I repent for gossiping, backbiting, talebearing, and speaking words that defile. I ask, dear Lord, that as You did with Isaiah, You would take the coals from Your altar and touch my lips. Let the fire of the Holy Spirit burn away iniquity in my heart and purge the sin of my mouth (Isa. 6:6–7). Let me speak with grace, seasoned with salt, that I will know how to answer with wisdom (Col. 4:6). Let me be a woman who is swift to hear, slow to speak, and slow to wrath (James 1:19).*

YOUR TURN

Use the space below to write out your own prayers and declarations.

_____

_____

_____

_____

_____

_____

_____

_____

_____

_____

_____

_____

_____

SEEK JUSTICE

SCRIPTURE

Many seek the ruler's favor, but justice for man comes from the LORD.

—PROVERBS 29:26, NKJV

Learn to do good; seek justice, relieve the oppressed; judge the fatherless, plead for the widow.

—ISAIAH 1:17

But let justice roll down like water, and righteousness like an ever-flowing stream.

—AMOS 5:24

He has told you, O man, what is good—and what does the LORD require of you, but to do justice and to love kindness, and to walk humbly with your God?

—MICAH 6:8

The Spirit of the Lord is upon Me, because He has anointed Me to preach the gospel to the poor; He has sent Me to heal the broken-hearted, to preach deliverance to the captives and recovery of sight to the blind, to set at liberty those who are oppressed.

—LUKE 4:18

Religion that is pure and undefiled before God, the Father, is this: to visit the fatherless and widows in their affliction and to keep oneself unstained by the world.

—JAMES 1:27

DECLARATIONS

I will seek justice and wholeness for all today (Isa. 1:17).

I will stand up for those who cannot stand on their own; I will be a voice for the voiceless (Prov. 31:8–9).

I resolve to feed the hungry and help the sick.

I will cry out for justice and peace, standing in the gap for those who need it.

I will speak against injustices.

I repent for injustices I have either knowingly or unknowingly perpetuated.

I will bring about God's justice through prayer (Isa. 58:2).

I will not be silent. I will open my mouth and speak the truth of the Lord.

I decree that every muzzle is removed from my mouth. By the power of Your Spirit let every muzzle of fear be removed from my mouth. I will be the voice of justice.

PRAYERS

God, Your Word promises to break in with power to those who embrace God's chosen fast (Isa. 58:6–12). Father, I pray that You will demonstrate Your power and justice for women worldwide. Let the light of Your power break forth like the morning. Let healing and deliverance be ignited to bring an end to the oppression of women and girls. Lord, righteousness and justice are the foundations of Your throne; let righteousness be extended to women. Lord, raise up deliverers who will execute justice that will help relieve women from the bondage that results from oppressive laws and social barriers that have been created over decades or centuries. Lord, let people be set in governmental positions who will give women a voice in the decision-making process. Let women all over the world be empowered to break the bonds of wickedness and heavy burdens. Let every yoke be destroyed.

Lord, give me creative ideas on how to help the oppressed. I will dream big and think outside the box. I believe change is possible, and I want to be a part of the solution. Lord, give me creative ways to raise awareness of women's issues.

Women in our world face many injustices. I am offering up a prayer here for one such issue: human trafficking. Be aware there are many other issues women face, including domestic violence, education inequality, health issues, and lack of economic empowerment. Pray the prayer below for human trafficking victims, but don't forget the other issues facing women today.

Lord, I pray for the end of human trafficking in all parts of the world. Lord, I pray that the light of Your glory will expose everything done in darkness. Let the issue of sex trafficking be brought to the forefront of our nation. Raise up voices for the voiceless victims. Let the public become educated about the issue. I pray for the righteous organizations who seek to bring an end to this social tragedy that they will have all of the resources to create social awareness and give ways to eradicate sex trafficking around the world. In Jesus's name I pray. Amen.

YOUR TURN

Use the space below to write out your own prayers and declarations.

_____

_____

_____

_____

_____

_____

_____

_____

_____

MAKE REQUESTS OF GOD

SCRIPTURE

And He said to them, Which of you who has a friend will go to him at midnight and will say to him, Friend, lend me three loaves [of bread], for a friend of mine who is on a journey has just come, and I have nothing to put before him; and he from within will answer, Do not disturb me; the door is now closed, and my children are with me in bed; I cannot get up and supply you [with anything]? I tell you, although he will not get up and supply him anything because he is his friend, yet because of his shameless persistence and insistence he will get up and give him as much as he needs. So I say to you, Ask and keep on asking and it shall be given you; seek and keep on seeking and you shall find; knock and keep on knocking and the door shall be opened to you. For everyone who asks and keeps on asking receives; and he who seeks and keeps on seeking finds; and to him who knocks and keeps on knocking, the door shall be opened.

—LUKE 11:5–10, AMPC

I will do whatever you ask in My name, that the Father may be glorified in the Son. If you ask anything in My name, I will do it.

—JOHN 14:13–14

Be anxious for nothing, but in everything, by prayer and supplication with gratitude, make your requests known to God. And the peace of God, which surpasses all understanding, will protect your hearts and minds through Christ Jesus.

—PHILIPPIANS 4:6–7

DECLARATIONS

God desires to give good things to me.

When I ask for things in the name of Jesus, my request will be answered (John 14:13–14).

I will make my requests known to God.

PRAYER

Father, I ask You for the salvation of the nations of the earth. You said that if we ask, You will give us the nations for our inheritance and the uttermost parts of the earth as our possessions. Lord, save our land. I humble myself. I come to You praying and crying out, for You will heal our land. I turn from my wicked ways. Lord, forgive us for being prideful and hard-hearted. I ask that You will come with revival and spiritual awakening. I ask that You will be merciful to us and bless us with Your presence. Let Your face shine upon us. Lord, we need Your wisdom in our land. I bind every antichrist devil that is loosed in the nations of the earth. Father, bring peace in our nations. Let Jesus, the Prince of Peace, be preached in every nation of the earth. Let the greater-works generation arise, those who will preach the gospel with power and demonstration, those who will not compromise Your standard of righteousness.

YOUR TURN

Use the space below to write out your own prayers and declarations.

_____

_____

_____

_____

_____

_____

_____

_____

_____

_____

_____

_____

_____

_____

SERVE OTHERS

SCRIPTURE

He who is greatest among you shall be your servant.

—MATTHEW 23:11

A new commandment I give to you, that you love one another, even as I have loved you, that you also love one another.

—JOHN 13:34

Be devoted to one another with brotherly love; prefer one another in honor.

—ROMANS 12:10

You, brothers, have been called to liberty. Only do not use liberty to give an opportunity to the flesh, but by love serve one another.

—GALATIANS 5:13

As everyone has received a gift, even so serve one another with it, as good stewards of the manifold grace of God.

—1 PETER 4:10

If anyone says, "I love God," and hates his brother, he is a liar. For whoever does not love his brother whom he has seen, how can he love God whom he has not seen? We have this commandment from Him: Whoever loves God must also love his brother.

—1 JOHN 4:20–21

DECLARATION

I will seek to serve God's people.

I will love my neighbors just as God has loved me (John 13:34).

I will always serve first, and see to the growth of individuals around me.

God has given me a gift, and I will use it to serve others and show His love to them (1 Pet. 4:10).

I will serve my brothers and sisters out of love for them and for God (Rom. 12:10).

PRAYER

Lord, open doors of opportunity for me to display Your love to my neighbor. Show me where I can bring righteousness, peace, and joy to this generation. Show me who needs prayer today, who needs a word of encouragement, or where I can volunteer. Lead me in these paths of righteousness.

YOUR TURN

Use the space below to write out your own prayers and declarations.

Part IV

GOING DEEPER

I T IS THE nature of the lion to roar—that is how it demonstrates its strength and power. As women of God, we have the Lion of Judah living inside us, and when we boldly speak the word God has given us, it is the Lion's roar.

God has a strategic plan for revival and reformation in which women will play a vital role. We are living in a time when God is calling and working through women to fulfill His redemptive plans for mankind. Some will be on the front lines of society, while others will live consecrated lives of prayer as their primary assignment.

God is empowering and equipping women with resolve and determination to find their calling and assignment in the Great Commission. God is calling ordinary women to His extraordinary work. Women will be a sign and wonder to this generation of the greatness and redeeming love of God. The Holy Spirit will empower women to do exploits and fulfill His purposes. Each woman's assignment is unique, but one aspect is always the same: she is on a mission with God to destroy the works of the devil in this generation.

The battle lines are being drawn, and there is a roar coming out of Zion that is feminine, strong, and full of compassion. This roar is from women anointed to preach the gospel of the kingdom, prophesy the word of the Lord, and pray prayers that touch heaven and change earth. Use the prayers and declarations in this section to embrace the wonderful calling of God. God is calling you to live as His ambassador among the nations, spreading His love and making an eternal difference in the lives of those in your sphere of influence.

PURSUE ANOINTING

SCRIPTURE

You love righteousness and hate wickedness; therefore God, your God, anointed you with the oil of gladness above your companions.

—PSALM 45:7

I will pour out My Spirit on all flesh; then your sons and your daughters will prophesy, your old men will dream dreams, and your young men will see visions.

—JOEL 2:28

I indeed baptize you with water to repentance, but He who is coming after me is mightier than I, whose shoes I am not worthy to carry. He will baptize you with the Holy Spirit and with fire.

—MATTHEW 3:11

Now He who establishes us with you in Christ and has anointed us is God, who also has sealed us and established the guarantee with the Spirit in our hearts.

—2 CORINTHIANS 1:21–22

But you have an anointing from the Holy One, and you know all things.... But the anointing which you have received from Him remains in you, and you do not need anyone to teach you. For as the same anointing teaches you concerning all things, and is truth, and is no lie, and just as it has taught you, remain in Him.

—1 JOHN 2:20, 27

DECLARATIONS

The Lord will anoint me to fulfill His calling for my life.

I decree that every muzzle is being broken from my mouth.

I will be bold in the Lord.

I will speak against injustice.

I will be a mouthpiece for the Lord.

I will pray and preach.

I will be a voice for the voiceless.

I will prophesy to my generation.

I will preach the Word of God with signs and wonders following.

I am a living flame of love.

PRAYERS

Father, I cry out to You for anointing, for an impartation of the spirit of grace and supplication. I believe that the effective prayers of the righteous make Your heavenly power available upon the earth. I lay aside my dreams and plans and press in to Your agenda and Your assignment for my life. I know that Your plans for me are good and not evil. Your plans for the earth are good and not evil. Lord, anoint me to partner with You in fulfilling the Great Commission. I find the hope of my future in Your presence. Let the power of the Holy Spirit fill every area of my life with Your wisdom and courage. Amen.

Lord, I ask that You will send Your fire into my life. Baptize my heart with the fire of Your love. Set Your seal of love upon my heart. Baptize me with the Holy Ghost and fire. Consume my entire being with the fire of Your presence. Lord, be a wall of fire around my life and the glory in my midst. Let me speak with tongues of fire, declaring Your Word to my generation. Let prophetic gifts be activated in my life. Give me a word of wisdom, a word of knowledge for the lost. Let me preach Your Word with fire and conviction. Let me move with gifts of healing and deliverance. Let my words be a demonstration of the Spirit and power! My faith will not be in the wisdom of men but in the power of God. Let me be a vessel of love and mercy to those who look for redemption.

Lord, I pray that You will awaken me to the call You have for my life. Remove any bondage of fear from my heart and mind. Let Your wisdom and courage rest upon me. Awaken me from slumber. Let me walk circumspectly in this hour. I loose myself from passivity and apathy. Let me be alert to Your voice. Let me be aware of Your purpose.

I thank You, Lord, that You are an extraordinary God and You will accomplish extraordinary things through me. I release myself from self-imposed limitations. I break every limitation that the enemy has placed upon my life and has kept me from meeting my full potential.

No longer will I be deceived and trapped by the traditions and opinions of men. For I was created for greatness! I was created to be God's glory carrier throughout the earth. I will arise and be radiant with the glory of the Lord. I will be a beaming lighthouse of hope for many who sit in gross darkness.

Lord, give me words of wisdom that will guide and influence many. I will not remain silent! I break every demonic conspiracy designed to keep me silent! I won't let past failures and disappointments keep me silent. I will open my mouth wide, and God, You will fill it.

God, give me ideas, insight, and concepts to bring deliverance to many. You have anointed me to impart grace to those in my sphere of influence. The words that I speak will release life to a hurting generation. I am not in this world by chance. I'm not in this decade by chance. I stir up and activate anointing through this prayer and declaration. In the name of Jesus, amen.

YOUR TURN

Use the space below to write out your own prayers and declarations.

CLAIM VICTORY

SCRIPTURE

For the LORD your God is He that goes with you, to fight for you against your enemies, to save you.

—DEUTERONOMY 20:4

I have told you these things so that in Me you may have peace. In the world you will have tribulation. But be of good cheer. I have overcome the world.

—JOHN 16:33

But thanks be to God, who gives us the victory through our Lord Jesus Christ!

—1 CORINTHIANS 15:57

Therefore take up the whole armor of God that you may be able to resist in the evil day, and having done all, to stand.

—EPHESIANS 6:13

DECLARATIONS

I am a victor and not a victim.

I am a bride of Christ; I will not live in defeat.

Jesus already won the victory.

I will pray for victory in my life.

I will put on the armor of God to bring about victory in my life (Eph. 6:11).

God's favor assures me of victory in any situation. The enemies of my destiny cannot triumph over me because God is with me (Ps. 44:3).

PRAYER

Father, help me to understand that I am a bride. Release Your power and glory upon my life. I am Your weapon of indignation. I will raise my voice to heaven until I see revival upon the earth. I will not be moved, shaken, or afraid of the gross darkness upon the earth. Let the light of Your glory fill the earth. Whatever adversity I may face, I choose to overcome by the power of Your love. Amen.

YOUR TURN

Use the space below to write out your own prayers and declarations.

_____

_____

_____

_____

_____

_____

_____

_____

BECOME A WATCHMAN

SCRIPTURE

Blessed is the man who hears me, watching daily at my gates, waiting at the posts of my doors.

—PROVERBS 8:34

Son of man, I have made you a watchman to the house of Israel. Whenever you hear the word from my mouth, then warn them from Me.

—EZEKIEL 3:17

I will stand at my watch and station myself on the watchtower; and I will keep watch to see what He will say to me, and what I will answer when I am reproved.

—HABAKKUK 2:1

DECLARATION

I will stand as a watchman and pray with perseverance.

I will watch and wait in the presence of the Lord to receive His instructions for this generation.

I will be a watchman for this generation.

PRAYER

Lord, I pray that You will set me as a watchman on the wall of prayer. Awaken my heart that I may cry out for my generation. Break my heart with the things that break Your heart. Lord, I don't want to be religious;

I want to be righteous. You said the effective, fervent prayer of the righteous makes tremendous power available. Let Your grace come upon me to watch and pray. Let me be sensitive to Your leading and prompting. Open my eyes, ears, and heart to perceive Your voice in this hour. Let me be connected to Your Spirit. I want to know the times and seasons of heaven. Let me connect to Your movements on the earth. Give me prophetic insight, discernment, and understanding. I break all prayerlessness off of my life. Your Word says that unless the Lord guards the city, the watchman stays awake in vain. Lord, I want to partner and co-labor with you. Set me on the watch You've ordained for me.

Your Turn

Use the space below to write out your own prayers and declarations.

_____

_____

_____

_____

_____

_____

_____

_____

INTERCEDE

SCRIPTURE

God was in Christ reconciling the world to Himself, not counting their sins against them, and has entrusted to us the message of reconciliation. So we are ambassadors for Christ, as though God were pleading through us. We implore you in Christ's stead: Be reconciled to God. God made Him who knew no sin to be sin for us, that we might become the righteousness of God in Him.

—2 CORINTHIANS 5:19–21

Pray in the Spirit always with all kinds of prayer and supplication. To that end be alert with all perseverance and supplication for all the saints.

—EPHESIANS 6:18

Therefore I exhort first of all that you make supplications, prayers, intercessions, and thanksgivings for everyone.

—1 TIMOTHY 2:1

In the days of His flesh, Jesus offered up prayers and supplications with loud cries and tears to Him who was able to save Him from death. He was heard because of His godly fear.

—HEBREWS 5:7

But He, because He lives forever, has an everlasting priesthood. Therefore He is able to save to the uttermost those who come to God through Him, because He at all times lives to make intercession for them.

—Hebrews 7:24–25

Declarations

I will love my neighbors as myself.

I will stand in the gap between the Lord and His mercy and the people and the nations in need of Him.

As an intercessor, I will identify myself with those I pray for, and I will plead their cause before the throne of God.

I will die to myself and give my life to others in prayer.

I will carry sin in prayer before the throne of grace to obtain mercy on behalf of the sinner.

I will intercede for individuals as well as for nations and cities.

Declarations and decrees for my family and future generations

I decree that the seed of the righteous shall be delivered from every evil plot against their destiny (Prov. 11:21).

I decree that the generation of the upright shall be blessed. Wealth and riches shall be in our house, and our righteousness shall endure forever (Ps. 112:3).

I break all limitations set by the enemy against my descendants' lives. I decree that they shall live and not die and shall declare the works of the Lord (Ps. 118:17).

I decree that no weapon formed against my family line shall prosper (Isa. 54:17).

I decree increase, expansion, and enlargement in the earth (Ps. 115:14–16).

I decree that God's everlasting mercy and peace shall rest upon my children (Isa. 54:13).

I decree that the goodness and mercy of the Lord shall follow my children all the days of their lives and my children shall dwell in the house of the Lord forever (Ps. 23:6).

I decree that my entire family shall be saved (Acts 16:31).

I decree that my descendants will be mighty on the earth (Ps. 112:2).

I decree that my children shall be taught of the Lord Jesus Christ (Isa. 54:13).

I decree that my children and my children's children will worship the name of the Lord Jesus Christ (Ps. 145:4).

Declarations and decrees for my city

I decree peace within the streets of my city (Deut. 20:10).

I decree that every assignment of violence and murder in my city will be broken (Ps. 55:9).

I decree that the river of God is flowing in my city (Ps. 46:4).

I decree that the voice of the Lord is heard in my city (Ps. 29:3).

I decree that my city belongs to Jesus, the great King (Ps. 48:2).

I decree that the Lord defends my city (Isa. 37:35).

I decree that the businesses in my city flourish like the grass of the earth (Ps. 72:16).

I decree that the Lord is watching over my city (Ps. 127:1).

I decree that the righteous have favor in my city (Prov. 11:10).

I decree that the Lord shall not forsake my city (Isa. 62:12).

I decree that revival will break out in my city.

I decree that the power of God is released in my city.

I decree that great joy is being released in my city (Acts 8:8).

I decree that a multitude of people will be saved in my city (Acts 18:10).

I decree that God is the builder and maker of my city (Heb. 11:10).

I decree that the spiritual name of my city is "THE LORD IS THERE" (Ezek. 48:35).

PRAYERS

Lord, I pray that You will make me a house of prayer. I believe the core identity of the church is to be a house of prayer for all nations. Lord, my heart's cry is, "Make me a house of prayer." Holy Spirit, fill me with the knowledge of Your will in wisdom and spiritual understanding. Lord, let me be a vessel used for

*Your glory. Give me the grace to labor in intercession
for the release of Your power to win the lost, revive the
church, and impact society with the gospel. I yield to
the Holy Spirit as He helps my infirmities and teaches
me to pray. Give me a steadfast, focused spirit. I desire
to offer my life as a drink offering to You. Let all the
days of my life serve Your purposes. Amen.*

*Lord, I decree that my country, my nation, and my
people belong to You. I ask, Father, for Your blessings on my nation. Let the beliefs and morals of Your
kingdom be established. Lord, I humble myself. I am
praying, seeking Your face, turning from my wicked
ways, and petitioning You to heal my land. I ask that
You will come and rain down righteousness in the land.
Let all wickedness and perversion be cleansed from
my land. Lord, awaken human hearts to Your love.
Let the power of conviction return to pulpits. Let the
preachers preach the gospel of Your kingdom.*

*Let there be an increased awareness of Your pres-
ence, God, and a new hunger for righteousness. Father,
I desire to see Your glory cover the earth like the waters
cover the sea. Let Your manifested presence return to
the earth.*

*Let revival break out in my country. Let the kingdom
of God break in with power. Let miracles, signs, and
wonders be released in my land. Let every manner of*

disease and sickness be healed. Let the fame of Jesus spread across this nation, from coast to coast. In Jesus's name I pray. Amen.

YOUR TURN

Use the space below to write out your own prayers and declarations.

_____

_____

_____

_____

_____

_____

_____

_____

_____

_____

_____

_____

_____

_____

_____

PURSUE REVIVAL

SCRIPTURE

Create in me a clean heart, O God, and renew a right spirit within me.

—PSALM 51:10

Will You not revive us again, that Your people may rejoice in You?

—PSALM 85:6

Therefore repent and be converted, that your sins may be wiped away, that times of refreshing may come from the presence of the Lord, and that He may send the One who previously was preached to you, Jesus Christ.

—ACTS 3:19–20

DECLARATIONS

I will humbly wait for and seek revival.

I will prepare myself through repentance for revival to happen in my life, my church, my community, and my nation.

The Lord will renew me and bring me to revival in Him (Ps. 51:10).

PRAYERS

Father, unite my heart to fear Your name. You said in Your Word that blessed are they who hunger and thirst for righteousness, for they shall be filled. Give me the gift of hunger. Empty me of religion and traditions of men. Break me out of the restraining mold of religion. Deliver me from dead, dry religion. My soul thirsts for You in a dry and weary land. I come to the well of Your Spirit and ask You to give me a drink. Give me living water. Spring up, O well, within me. Let the fountain of water spring up into a fountain of everlasting life.

Holy Spirit, we need You! There is no revival without You! I ask that You will release unified prayer throughout the earth. Let the spirit of grace and supplication ignite human hearts with a passion for the living God. Raise up a generation to cry out day and night like Anna and give You no rest until the knowledge of the glory of the Lord covers the earth as the waters cover the sea. Let a genuine spirit of prayer produced by the Holy Spirit be released upon this generation.

Father, we ask for a continuous revival in the land. Let Your presence and Your glory cover the earth as the waters cover the sea. Lord, we ask that You restore Your power in the church. Let miracles, signs, and wonders be released. Let the power of the Lord be present to heal. Heal families, relationships, and broken hearts. Let revival start in the heart of every believer. Let there be new commitment to see reformation in the church.

Let new churches be planted. Let new ministries be birthed to meet the needs of this generation.

YOUR TURN

Use the space below to write out your own prayers and declarations.

_____

_____

_____

_____

_____

_____

_____

_____

_____

_____

_____

_____

_____

_____

_____

_____

CALL ON THE HOLY SPIRIT

SCRIPTURE

I will pray the Father, and He will give you another Counselor, that He may be with you forever: the Spirit of truth, whom the world cannot receive, for it does not see Him, neither does it know Him. But you know Him, for He lives with you, and will be in you.

—JOHN 14:16–17

But the Counselor, the Holy Spirit, whom the Father will send in My name, will teach you everything and remind you of all that I told you.

—JOHN 14:26

When suddenly there came a sound from heaven like the rushing of a violent tempest blast, and it filled the whole house in which they were sitting. And there appeared to them tongues resembling fire, which were separated and distributed and which settled on each one of them. And they were all filled (diffused throughout their souls) with the Holy Spirit and began to speak in other (different, foreign) languages (tongues), as the Spirit kept giving them clear and loud expression [in each tongue in appropriate words].

—ACTS 2:2–4, AMPC

Likewise, the Spirit helps us in our weaknesses, for we do not know what to pray for as we ought, but the

Spirit Himself intercedes for us with groanings too deep for words. He who searches the hearts knows what the mind of the Spirit is, because He intercedes for the saints according to the will of God. We know that all things work together for good to those who love God, to those who are called according to His purpose.

—ROMANS 8:26–28

DECLARATIONS

The Spirit that raised Christ from the dead lives inside of me!

The power of the Spirit can be applied to every circumstance I face.

I will listen to the voice of the Holy Spirit as He reveals plans God has put in my spirit.

PRAYER

Father, I ask that You pour out the spirit of grace and supplication upon my life. Let me pray effective, fervent prayers. Holy Spirit, help me to intercede unceasingly for the lost. Let the grace of God fill my life. Help me to pray Your heart and mind for cities and nations. Infuse my prayers with grace. Restore the spirit of supplication to Your church. Holy Spirit, teach us how to pray prayers of supplication and intercession that we may live godly and peaceable lives in all godliness and reverence upon the earth. Father, I ask You to activate and release a similar grace upon a whole generation of women. Let us pray until the knowledge of the glory of the Lord covers the earth.

YOUR TURN

Use the space below to write out your own prayers and declarations.

_____

_____

_____

_____

_____

_____

_____

_____

_____

_____

_____

_____

_____

_____

_____

_____

_____

ENGAGE IN SPIRITUAL WARFARE

SCRIPTURE

No weapon that is formed against you shall prosper.

—ISAIAH 54:17

The weapons of our warfare are not carnal, but mighty through God to the pulling down of strongholds.

—2 CORINTHIANS 10:4

Be strong in the Lord and in the power of His might. Put on the whole armor of God that you may be able to stand against the schemes of the devil. For our fight is not against flesh and blood, but against principalities, against powers, against the rulers of the darkness of this world, and against spiritual forces of evil in the heavenly places. Therefore take up the whole armor of God that you may be able to resist in the evil day, and having done all, to stand. Stand therefore, having your waist girded with truth, having put on the breastplate of righteousness, having your feet fitted with the readiness of the gospel of peace, and above all, taking the shield of faith, with which you will be able to extinguish all the fiery arrows of the evil one. Take the helmet of salvation and the sword of the Spirit, which is the word of God.

—EPHESIANS 6:10–17

Therefore submit yourselves to God. Resist the devil, and he will flee from you.

—James 4:7

DECLARATIONS

When I submit to God, Satan will flee.

I will partner with the Spirit to stand in the gap and intercede for the souls of our nations and bring the Lord's will to the earth.

With the armor of God, I can withstand evil sources.

PRAYER

Lord, make me a warrior. Teach my hands to fight and my fingers to war. I make a decision to put on the whole armor of God that I may stand against every wile, trick, or trap of the devil. I securely fasten my heart and mind with the belt of truth. I am a champion of truth. I will live in the truth of Your Word. The truth of Your Word will protect me from all deception and seduction. I cover my heart with the breastplate of righteousness, protecting me from all temptation I may face in the world. I am a preacher of righteousness, proclaiming Your truth to the world. Your righteousness and justice are the foundations of Your throne. I pray that You will let justice roll like a river in the earth. I put on my shoes of peace that I will be a peacemaker wherever I go. I have peace because You are the Prince of Peace. I will not be fearful or anxious.

I choose to trust You. I take up the shield of faith to quench every dart of the enemy. I rebuke all doubt and deception. I will be bold and strong in the Lord and the power of His might. I love what God loves and hate what He hates. I fight with Him, advancing His kingdom on the earth. I put on the helmet of salvation to protect my mind. I will live in the power of my salvation. I take up the sword of the Spirit, which is the daily Word of God for my life.

YOUR TURN

Use the space below to write out your own prayers and declarations.

DISCERN THE TIMES

SCRIPTURE

To everything there is a season, a time for every purpose under heaven: a time to be born, and a time to die; a time to plant, and a time to uproot what is planted; a time to kill, and a time to heal; a time to break down, and a time to build up; a time to weep, and a time to laugh; a time to mourn, and a time to dance; a time to cast away stones, and a time to gather stones; a time to embrace, and a time to refrain from embracing; a time to gain, and a time to lose; a time to keep, and a time to cast away; a time to tear, and a time to sew; a time to keep silence, and a time to speak; a time to love, and a time to hate; a time of war, and a time of peace.

—ECCLESIASTES 3:1–8

There is an appropriate time for every matter and deed.
—ECCLESIASTES 3:17

It is He who changes the times and seasons; He removes kings and sets up kings.

—DANIEL 2:21

And let us not be weary in well doing: for in due season we shall reap, if we faint not.

—GALATIANS 6:9, KJV

Preach the word, be ready in season and out of season, reprove, rebuke, and exhort, with all patience and teaching.

—2 Timothy 4:2

Declarations

God knows the right time. Through time I will mature; when it is His time, I will be ready for His call.

When my calling feels overwhelming, I will keep saying "yes" to God.

I am empowered by the Holy Spirit to fulfill my God-given destiny in His time.

Through learning to discern the times and seasons, I will align my actions with the Lord's plans.

I will embrace the testing of God because I know it will prepare me to move into my calling at the right time.

Prayers

Lord, I pray that You will make me a woman who understands time and seasons. Enlighten the eyes of my understanding. Help me balance the seasons of my life. There is a season and time to every purpose. Thank You, Lord, for the Issachar anointing, the anointing to understand the times (2 Chron. 12:32). *Lord, I want to do everything You've assigned to my life. Let the spirit of revelation and understanding be released in my life.*

I decree that I am a woman who walks in total synchronization with the time clock of heaven. I loose myself from time-delay spirits. I decree divine acceleration in my life. I will no longer lag behind, neither will I get ahead of You. I will be in the right place at the right time.

I decree divine alignment for my assignment. I decree alignment in my thought patterns. I decree alignment in my time. I will not squander time. I will maximize every moment for the purposes of the Lord.

Lord, I give You permission to remove anything that will delay Your purposes in my life. Remove anything that will hinder Your call on my life, including relationships or people. Let me attract the people who will propel me into Your purposes for my life. Lord, send instructors and mentors who have words of wisdom and instructions in due season for my life.

Thank You, Lord, for appointing my days and ordering my steps. I surrender to Your timing. In Jesus's name I pray. Amen.

Lord, Your Word says that the sons of Issachar had understanding of the times and knew what Israel should do (1 Chron. 12:32). *I ask that You release that same grace upon my life. I decree that I am a woman who understands the times in my life. I will move in complete synchronization with Your timing.*

Lord, give me the wisdom like the sons of Issachar to understand the times in which I live. Lord, I ask that You keep me in perfect time with You. Let me not get ahead of Your process. I ask for grace to endure.

Lord, I also pray that I learn the times and season of my generation. I desire to understand them. I want to understand my culture. Lord, I ask that You would give me heavenly insight to effectively engage my culture. In Jesus's name, amen.

YOUR TURN

Use the space below to write out your own prayers and declarations.

_____

_____

_____

_____

_____

_____

_____

_____

_____

_____

_____

_____

DISCERN SPIRITS

SCRIPTURE

"Give Your servant therefore an understanding heart to judge Your people, that I may discern between good and bad, for who is able to judge among so great a people?" It pleased the Lord that Solomon had asked this. God said to him, "Because you have asked this and have not asked for yourself long life or riches or the lives of your enemies, but have asked for yourself wisdom so that you may have discernment in judging, I now do according to your words. I have given you a wise and an understanding heart."

—1 KINGS 3:9–12

To one is given by the Spirit the word of wisdom, to another the word of knowledge by the same Spirit, . . . to another discerning of spirits.

—1 CORINTHIANS 12:8–10

But solid food belongs to those who are of full age, that is, those who by reason of use have their senses exercised to discern both good and evil.

—HEBREWS 5:14, NKJV

Do not believe every spirit, but test the spirits to see whether they are from God, because many false prophets have gone out into the world.

—1 JOHN 4:1

169

DECLARATIONS

I will pray for the gift of discerning spirits so the evil one cannot use the evil spirits of seduction and deception against me.

The Lord will give the good gifts I ask for.

God will give me the wisdom to discern spirits when I ask in His name.

PRAYERS

Lord, Your Word declares that if I ask You for a gift, You will give it to me. So, Lord, I ask You for the gift of discerning of spirits. Let the supernatural power of the Holy Spirit be activated in me to detect the realm of the spirits and their activities. Let me have grace to discern between good and evil. Let me have spiritual insight to Your plans and supernatural revelation of the plans of the enemy. Empower me with Your supernatural ability to discern and stop the plans of the enemy against my life and the lives of others. Give me a wise and understanding heart that I might discern justice. (See Matthew 7:7–11; James 1:17; 1 Kings 3:9–11.)

Lord, give me a piece of Your heart for my generation. Help me to be a woman of compassion. Break my heart with the things that break Your heart. Take away my

stony heart and give me a heart of flesh. God, I repent of all hardness of heart that makes me indifferent to the plight of men. Father, I pray that You will make me sensitive to the moving of the Holy Spirit. Your Word says that manifestation of the Spirit is given to each one. I ask that You give me the gift of discerning of spirits. Enlighten the eyes of my understanding. Remove every scale from my eyes that I may see by Your Spirit. Awaken my ear so I might hear and perceive what You are saying and doing. I break off all blind, deaf, and dumb spirits. I will be a woman who hears Your voice. Make me a woman of vision and insight. Lord, empower me to pray effective, fervent prayers. Make me a house of prayer for all nations!

YOUR TURN

Use the space below to write out your own prayers and declarations.

ANSWER THE CALL OF PROPHECY

SCRIPTURE

For who has stood in the counsel of the LORD and has perceived and heard His word? Who has given heed to His word and listened to it?…But if they had stood in My counsel and had caused My people to hear My words, then they would have turned them from their evil way and from the evil of their deeds.

—JEREMIAH 23:18, 22

Surely the Lord GOD does nothing without revealing His purpose to His servants the prophets.

—AMOS 3:7

Follow after love and desire spiritual gifts, but especially that you may prophesy. For he who speaks in an unknown tongue does not speak to men, but to God…But he who prophesies speaks to men for their edification and exhortation and comfort…I desire that you all speak in tongues, but even more that you prophesy.

—1 CORINTHIANS 14:1–5

DECLARATIONS

The Lord will guide me with His voice; I need only listen.

I will stand and wait to hear the message God wants to deliver to me; I will wait for His counsel.

Lord, I declare that as I open my mouth, You will fill it with Your words (Ps. 81:10).

I will prophesy to the dry bones in my generation.

I will prophesy life and hope to the hopeless (Ezek. 37).

Let my eyes be open to see from Your perspective (1 Cor. 2:9).

Let my ears be open to hear Your truth.

Let my heart be pure to perceive Your will.

Lord, put Your eternal truth in my heart (Eccles. 3:11).

Prayers

Let the spirit of wisdom and revelation rest upon my life. Lord, You are the God who reveals secrets; reveal Your secrets unto me (Amos 3:7). Let the eyes of my understanding be enlightened; let my heart be flooded with light. Open my eyes so that I might behold wondrous things from Your law. I rebuke spiritual blindness. Let me understand the mystery of Your kingdom. Let me receive and understand Your wisdom. I want to know Your thoughts and mind for my life.

Lord, I believe that You are the Good Shepherd, and I am Your sheep. I believe Your Word that says I can hear and know Your voice. Your sheep know Your voice and follow You. I will not follow a stranger's

voice (John 10:4–5). *Father, I humble myself as one of Your sheep and ask that You activate Your voice in my heart. I desire to hear Your voice on a greater level. Let the gift of prophecy be activated in my life. I desire to hear and release Your voice to my generation. By faith I stir up the gift of prophecy* (2 Tim. 1:6). *I rebuke all spirits of fear that will hinder the flow of the Spirit in my life. Open my ears hear to hear Your voice. Awaken my ear morning by morning to Your gentle promptings. Give me the tongue of the learned that I might speak a word in season to those who are weary* (Isa. 50:4). *Lord, I open the doors of my heart that You may come in and teach me. I desire to dine with You. I desire that You will teach me Your ways. I desire that You will give me insight into things that are going on around me. I desire that You will give me the things I need to say for the task ahead of me.*

YOUR TURN

Use the space below to write out your own prayers and declarations.

LIVE IN THE POWER
OF THE SPIRIT

SCRIPTURE

God has spoken once, twice have I heard this: that power belongs to God.

—PSALM 62:11

The Lord gives the word [of power]; the women who bear and publish [the news] are a great host.

—PSALM 68:11, AMPC

They were astonished at His teaching, for His word was with authority.... They were all amazed and said among themselves, "What a word this is! For with authority and power He commands the unclean spirits, and they come out."

—LUKE 4:32, 36

God anointed Jesus of Nazareth with the Holy Spirit and with power, who went about doing good and healing all who were oppressed by the devil, for God was with Him.

—ACTS 10:38

My speech and my preaching was not with enticing words of man's wisdom, but in demonstration of the Spirit and of power, so that your faith should not stand in the wisdom of men, but in the power of God.

—1 CORINTHIANS 2:4–5

DECLARATIONS

I break every limitation and barrier set up in my life by the devil.

I break all stagnation and deformity in my life.

I break all small-mindedness. I will think big and dream big.

I will break out on the left and the right. I will advance in my call and move forward in my destiny.

I decree enlargement in my life.

I decree enlargement to my ministry.

I decree enlargement and new territory to preach the gospel. There is no speech or language where my voice will not be heard. My mouth will be enlarged over my enemies (1 Sam. 2:1).

I will allow the Lord to enlarge my heart so I can run in the way of His commandments (Ps. 119:32).

The Lord will deliver me from fear and a low opinion of myself.

The Lord will enlarge my steps so I can receive His wealth and prosperity.

I receive deliverance and enlargement for my life and my children (Esther 4:14).

Prayers

In the name of Jesus, I will think the thoughts of God. I will dream with God. No longer will I consider myself least and smallest because I am a woman. I can do all things through Christ who strengthens me. I loose myself from fear and settling for less than what I deserve.

In the name of Jesus, I break through every glass ceiling. I prophesy to the borders of my life: increase! I cast down every demonic imagination and argument against the knowledge of Christ. I will not be double-minded about my call! I am a conqueror through Jesus Christ.

Lord, Your Word says that as a man thinks in his heart, so is he (Prov. 23:7). *Let me think on Your thoughts toward me. For Your thoughts are as numerous as the sand on the seashore.*

I rebuke every spirit of withdrawal in the name of Jesus. I will not retreat from the purposes of the Lord. I will move forward in the plans of God. I decree that I will not accomplish my call in my own strength. It's not by might nor power but by the Spirit of the Lord that every mountain shall be removed from my life. I shout, "Grace, grace," to the mountain of prejudice,

intimidation, and fear. God, give me Your heart for my assignment. Give me Your perspective that I might be Your mouthpiece in the earth. I will stand up against injustice. I am the righteousness of God, and I am bold as a lion. I am fearless in the face of danger. I will preach the Word. I will go wherever You send me. In Jesus's name I pray. Amen.

YOUR TURN

Use the space below to write out your own prayers and declarations.

_____

_____

_____

_____

_____

_____

_____

_____

_____

_____

_____

_____

_____

FIND FAVOR IN GOD'S EYES

SCRIPTURE

For You, Lord, will bless the righteous; You surround him with favor like a shield.

—Psalm 5:12

For His anger endures but a moment, in His favor is life; weeping may endure for a night, but joy comes in the morning.

—Psalm 30:5

For the Lord God is a sun and shield; the Lord will give favor and glory, for no good thing will He withhold from the one who walks uprightly.

—Psalm 84:11

For whoever finds me finds life, and will obtain favor of the Lord.

—Proverbs 8:35

DECLARATIONS

I proclaim that this is the year of the favor of the Lord! This is the set time for the favor of the Lord to be manifested in my life.

I am growing in stature, wisdom is increasing, and favor is being multiplied to me.

Let the favor of the Lord open doors to my assignment that no man can shut.

I receive preferential treatment, goodwill, and advantages toward success in every area of my life.

Let the favor of the Lord surround me as a shield.

Let the spirit of favor compel men to assist me in fulfilling my destiny.

The kings of the earth are extending the scepter of favor toward me, and I have all the financial resources to accomplish the purpose of God.

Leaders and heads of state show kind regards toward me. Their hearts are open to hear and grant my request.

I have favor with everyone assigned to my destiny.

I receive life and favor of the Most High God.

God surrounds and protects me with favor like a shield (Ps. 5:12).

The Lord is a sun and shield. He bestows favor and honor, and no good thing does He withhold from me.

I actively seek and live by God's wisdom; therefore, I am highly favored and esteemed in the sight of God and men.

God's favor brings promotion and causes me to increase daily.

My enemies cannot triumph over me because the Lord has favored me.

PRAYER

Lord, my prayer to You is for a time of favor. In Your abundant, faithful love, God, answer me with Your sure mercies. Lord, grant me favor in every situation assigned to restrict my purpose and hinder my advancement. Lord, cause every wicked device to be broken, but by Your goodness allow me to obtain favor. Lord, I thank You for favor to complete my assignment in the earth. You are connecting me with key people who will unlock and advance Your purpose in my life. Lord, let my life carry the fragrance of favor. Lord, You are my sun and shield; You bestow upon me favor and honor. There is no good thing withheld from me. Lord, I thank You for supernatural increase and promotion. Let Your presence and Your care preserve and protect me. In Jesus's name I pray. Amen.

Your Turn

Use the space below to write out your own prayers and declarations.

ACTIVATE A SPIRIT OF INFLUENCE

SCRIPTURE

You are the light of the world. A city that is set on a hill cannot be hidden. Neither do men light a candle and put it under a basket, but on a candlestick. And it gives light to all who are in the house. Let your light so shine before men that they may see your good works and glorify your Father who is in heaven.

—MATTHEW 5:14–16

Therefore let us no longer pass judgment on one another, but rather determine not to put a stumbling block or an obstacle in a brother's way.

—ROMANS 14:13

Let your speech always be with grace, seasoned with salt, that you may know how you should answer everyone.

—COLOSSIANS 4:6

In all things showing yourself to be a pattern of good works; in doctrine showing integrity, reverence, incorruptibility.

—TITUS 2:7, NKJV

DECLARATIONS

I decree that I am a change agent.

I have wisdom, insight, and influence with the next generation.

I decree that I am aligned for my assignment.

I am fearfully and wonderfully made in God's image.

I will find the place where my influence will operate.

PRAYER

Father, I thank You that You are awakening influence inside of me. Awaken me to my sphere of influence. Remove the scales from my eyes that I may see those I've been designed to touch. Lord, You've given me unique gifts and talents to affect those around me. Let the gifts that You have given me make room for me in the earth. Let me have creativity and free expression of my gifts. Let me connect with those who will train and equip me. I will start where I am, while pressing in to all that You have for me. I will not draw back in fear. I will impart that which I have to those assigned to my life.

Lord, send me to those who will think I'm wonderful. Send me to those who have an ear to hear my voice.

I will find my wonderful place. In Jesus's name, amen.

YOUR TURN

Use the space below to write out your own prayers and declarations.

_____

_____

_____

_____

_____

_____

_____

_____

_____

_____

_____

_____

_____

_____

_____

_____

_____

_____

_____

_____

Part V

BECOMING A WOMAN OF GOD

D ESTINY BEGINS WITH a seed, and every one of us has the seed of destiny inside us. The Bible says that God has "planted eternity [a sense of divine purpose] in the human heart [a mysterious longing which nothing under the sun can satisfy, except God]" (Eccl. 3:11, AMP). This longing is toward a purpose or destiny that is so big we cannot fathom it. It is beyond our comprehension. But there is a part for us to discover, act on, and reap from.

God is looking for those who will plant and cultivate the seed of destiny He planted within them. He is most interested in promoting women who are fruitful—those who will not only talk about it, but will also be about it, those who are ready to do something. If you know that the Lord is calling you into your destiny, you cannot afford to remain in the company of people who do nothing. Like the limitations they place upon themselves, they will attempt to imprison you with their expectations of who you should be—things that they think are dictated by color, gender, social class, or economic status. But you do not need to fall victim to this mentality, becoming hitched to societal balls and chains.

The awareness of the purpose and destiny of God

provides all the force you need to stand against opposition. That awareness will ground you when resources don't line up with the vision. It will give you the faith and courage you need to step into the vision. Provision, favor, and finances will come when you start moving in your calling. People will help when you start walking in your purpose.

Woman of God, it is time for you to do what God determined for you before you were born. There are people and places waiting for you to arise and embrace your destiny. God did not design you to live a mundane, mediocre life. Use the prayers, scriptures, and declarations in this section to allow the Lord to unlock greatness inside you. Don't allow racism, sexism, or classism defeat and define you. The Lord is releasing tenacity and determination in your heart to live out your destiny. Receive it! You are a world changer.

UNDERSTAND YOUR IDENTITY AS A WOMAN OF GOD

SCRIPTURE

So God created man in His own image; in the image of God He created him; male and female He created them.

—GENESIS 1:27

You brought my inner parts into being; You wove me in my mother's womb. I will praise you, for You made me with fear and wonder; marvelous are Your works, and You know me completely.

—PSALM 139:13–14

Before I formed you in the womb I knew you; and before you were born I sanctified you, and I ordained you a prophet to the nations.

—JEREMIAH 1:5

For we are His workmanship, created in Christ Jesus for good works, which God prepared beforehand, so that we should walk in them.

—EPHESIANS 2:10

Let not yours be the [merely] external adorning with [elaborate] interweaving and knotting of the hair, the wearing of jewelry, or changes of clothes; but let it be the inward adorning and beauty of the hidden person of the heart, with the incorruptible and unfading charm of a gentle and peaceful spirit, which [is not anxious or wrought up, but] is very precious in the sight of God.

—1 PETER 3:3–4, AMP

DECLARATIONS

I was made for more.

I declare in the name of Jesus that I will arise as a mighty woman of God from the depression and prostration in which circumstances have kept me—I will rise to a new life!

I declare that this is a season when old things are passing away and all things are being made new in my life. God is calling me to active duty in His heavenly army.

I declare that this is a time when the heavenly Father will make all of my God-given dreams and aspirations come to fruition.

I declare that this is my time and season to accomplish and live in God's ordained purpose and destiny.

I declare that I will arise from fear and embrace the courage of the Lord.

PRAYER

O Lord, I thank You that You are an extraordinary God who will accomplish extraordinary things through me. I release myself from self-imposed limitations. I break every limitation that the enemy has placed upon my life. Lord, Your Word says, "Loose thyself... O captive daughter of Zion" (Isa. 52:2, KJV), *and in the name of Jesus, I loose myself from every limitation, barrier, obstruction, and demonic mind-set that has kept me from meeting my full potential. No longer will I be deceived and trapped by traditions and the opinions of men. I was created for greatness! I was created to be God's glory carrier throughout the earth.*

I will arise and be radiant with the glory of the Lord. Let the glory of the Lord shine through me. I am a beaming lighthouse of hope for many who sit in gross darkness.

Lord, give me words of wisdom that will guide and influence many. I will not remain silent! I break every demonic conspiracy designed to keep me silent! I won't let past failures and disappointments keep me silent. I will open my mouth wide, and God will fill it.

God, give me ideas, insight, and concepts to bring deliverance to many. You have anointed me to impart grace to those in my sphere of influence. The words I speak will release life to a hurting generation.

I am not in this world by chance. I'm not in this decade by chance. I'm not reading this book by chance. I embrace my inner and outer beauty. I decree that the power of femininity is being awakened inside of me.

Lord, Your Word says that You will make everything beautiful in its time. I submit my life and destiny to Your making and timing. I surrender all ambition and striving to You. I ask that You will give me grace to endure the purifying process. I realize that the race is not given to the swift or strong but to the one who endures to the end.

I choose to submit to the inner dealings of the Holy Spirit. Lord, remove anything from my heart that will hinder my destiny. A broken and contrite heart You will not despise. Cleanse me of all pride, arrogance, and fear. Let love and kindness flow from my heart.

The world has many definitions of beauty, but, Lord, I want to radiate the authentic beauty of the kingdom. Favor can be deceitful and beauty vain, but a woman who fears the Lord, she will be praised. I am a woman who fears the Lord. I will develop the traits of kindness and humility.

Lord, remove all mixture of the negative life experience from my behavior and values. I choose to be better and not bitter. Let the fire of the Holy Ghost purge away bitterness, anger, frustration, and disappointment.

I submit to the anointing of myrrh. Let the oil of myrrh cleanse every wrinkle and blemish in my character. I am a sweet-smelling fragrance and preservative in the rotting and decaying world around me. I will release the fragrance of joy, love, and hope to a dying world.

Thank You, God, for being faithful to complete this work in me. In Jesus's name, amen.

YOUR TURN

Use the space below to write out your own prayers and declarations.

_____

_____

_____

_____

_____

_____

_____

_____

_____

_____

_____

_____

_____

_____

_____

_____

_____

_____

_____

_____

_____

BECOME A WOMAN OF VIRTUE AND EXCELLENCE

SCRIPTURE

And now, my daughter, do not fear. I will do for you all that you request, for all the people of my town know that you are a virtuous woman.

—RUTH 3:11, NKJV

Who can find a virtuous woman? For her worth is far above rubies. The heart of her husband safely trusts in her, so that he will have no lack of gain. She will do him good and not evil all the days of her life. She seeks wool and flax, and works willingly with her hands. She is like the merchant ships, she brings her food from afar. She also rises while it is yet night, and gives food to her household, and a portion to her maidens. She considers a field and buys it; with the fruit of her hands she plants a vineyard. She clothes herself with strength, and strengthens her arms. She perceives that her merchandise is good; her candle does not go out by night. She lays her hands to the spindle, and her hands hold the distaff. She stretches out her hand to the poor; yes, she reaches forth her hands to the needy. She is not afraid of the snow for her household, for all her household are clothed with scarlet. She makes herself coverings of tapestry; her clothing is silk and purple. Her husband is known in the gates, when he sits among the elders of the land. She makes fine linen and sells it, and delivers sashes to the merchant. Strength and honor are her clothing, and she will rejoice in time to come. She opens her mouth with wisdom, and in her tongue is the teaching of kindness. She looks well to the ways of her household, and does not eat the bread of idleness. Her children rise up and call her blessed; her husband also, and he praises her: "Many daughters have done virtuously, but you excel them all." Charm is deceitful, and beauty is vain, but a woman who fears the LORD, she shall be praised. Give her of the fruit of her hands, and let her own works praise her in the gates.

—PROVERBS 31:10–31

DECLARATIONS

With the Lord's help, I will seek to be a virtuous woman.

I will pray that my virtuous reputation precede me.

I will support and show loyalty to my spouse, my children, and my loved ones (Ruth 2:11).

I will take initiative to get done what must be done (Ruth 2:2).

I am a valuable contributor, and I will see myself as such.

The joy of the Lord is my strength; I will remind myself of this when joy is hard to find (Neh. 8:10).

As a virtuous woman, I will seek to care for other women suffering in poverty (Prov. 31:20).

God has given me authority, and I will use it to follow God's call on my life.

The Lord has equipped me to live with excellence and humility.

I will speak wisdom and kindness (Prov. 31:26).

I will clothe myself with the strength the Lord has given to me (Prov. 31:17).

God has equipped and empowered me with the Holy Spirit to be a virtuous woman.

I will seek to be diligent and not slothful.

I will try to be the wise woman who recognizes opportunities and takes them (Prov. 12:27).

As a godly woman of virtue and excellence, I will be diligent, faithful, patient, and hardworking.

Lord, where You go, I will go.

PRAYER

Lord, You said in Your Word that the hand of the diligent shall rule. I receive a diligent spirit. I break off all slothful spirits from my life. Let Your hand come upon and empower me to be a woman of excellence. Father, clothe me with dignity and strength. Lord, teach me how to walk in humility in a world full of pride and arrogance. I humble myself under Your mighty hand, and You will exalt me as a virtuous woman. Father, give me creative ideas to start my own business. Give me the power to get wealth that I may establish Your covenant in the earth. Make me a voice for the voiceless.

YOUR TURN

Use the space below to write out your own prayers and declarations.

NURTURE

SCRIPTURE

The man called his wife's name Eve because she was the mother of all the living.

—GENESIS 3:20

Train up a child in the way he should go, and when he is old he will not depart from it.

—PROVERBS 22:6

Her children rise up and call her blessed; her husband also, and he praises her.

—PROVERBS 31:28

DECLARATIONS

As a woman, I was created and am called to nurture life.

I will devote myself to nurturing those around me who need love and care.

PRAYER

Lord, I pray that Your purpose for the next generation will be fulfilled. I decree that the next generation will arise in power, authority, and influence to possess the gates of their enemies (Gen. 22:17–18).

I bind all spirits of premature death and destruction. I decree long life over the next generation.

I pray for academic excellence and social impact to rest upon the next generation. I decree that the next generation of Christian leaders will resist all false doctrines such as humanism, secularism, and hedonism. They will know the truth, preach the truth, and live out the truth of the Lord Jesus (Dan. 1:4–5).

I decree that the seed of the righteous shall be delivered from all wicked and ungodly attractions at work to seduce them into an alternative lifestyle (Prov. 11:21).

Lord, I ask that You will encounter the next generation with dreams and visions and an overwhelming awareness of Your love and presence.

Let peace blanket the hearts and minds of the next generation. Let the God of peace crush fear under their feet (Isa. 54:13–14).

I decree that the next generation will grow in the ways of God. Let them be strengthened in spiritual things. I decree that the next generation will increase in wisdom, stature, and the favor of God (Luke 2:40, 52).

I decree that the next generation will be like arrows of the Lord. They will bring forth deliverance to the nations of the earth (Ps. 127:3–5).

Lord, I ask that You will preserve the heritage of the gospel through the next generation! In Jesus's name I pray. Amen.

YOUR TURN

Use the space below to write out your own prayers and declarations.

BUILD A STRONG MARRIAGE

SCRIPTURE

God created man in his own image, in the image of God created he him; male and female created he them. And God blessed them, and God said unto them, Be fruitful, and multiply, and replenish the earth, and subdue it: and have dominion over the fish of the sea, and over the fowl of the air, and over every living thing that moveth upon the earth.

—GENESIS 1:27–28, KJV

Then the rib which the LORD God had taken from man, He made into a woman, and He brought her to the man. Then Adam said, "This is now bone of my bones and flesh of my flesh; she will be called Woman, for she was taken out of Man." Therefore a man will leave his father and his mother and be joined to his wife, and they will become one flesh.

—GENESIS 2:22–24

Whoever finds a wife finds a good thing, and obtains favor of the LORD.

—PROVERBS 18:22

Who can find a virtuous woman? For her worth is far above rubies.

—PROVERBS 31:10

But from the beginning of the creation, God "made them male and female." "For this cause shall a man leave his father and mother, and cleave to his wife, and the two shall be one flesh." So then they are no longer two, but one flesh. What therefore God has joined together, let not man put asunder.

—MARK 10:6–9

DECLARATIONS

I cancel every assignment of darkness against my marriage.

I bind any evil, seducing spirit trying to attack my husband, in Jesus's name.

I pursue, overtake, and recover my marriage from the grip of marriage-destroying spirits.

I rebuke every marriage-destroying spirit in the name of Jesus.

I decree that what God has joined together, no one will separate.

I release the gift of leadership upon my husband's life. Let the wisdom of Solomon rest upon him.

I decree that my husband is a man of authority and he walks in the authority of the kingdom.

I rebuke every selfish spirit.

I rebuke the accuser of the brothers and finger pointing. I decree that we will be quick to forgive each other.

PRAYERS

For the married woman

Lord, let mutual love and respect flow in my marriage. Let my husband lead our family according to the purposes of the Lord. Let grace and love flow in our home. Let our home be a place where the glory of the Lord dwells. Let unity and oneness flow in our marriage covenant. I decree that my husband and I are one flesh; therefore, we are no longer two but one (Matt. 19:6). Let us be tenderhearted toward each other. I rebuke the spirit of hardness of heart. I rebuke the spirit of divorce. Father, bless our marriage.

For the single woman

"It is not good that the man should be alone; I will make him a helper fit for him" (Gen. 2:18, RSV). Father, I thank You that You are restoring male and female relationships in the body of Christ. Your Word says that two are better than one. I pray for divine connection and men with pure hearts to be drawn to me. I loose myself from pains from the past. Lord, the power of Your blood cleanses my heart from all bitterness. I will be a woman of authority and submit to men in authority.

YOUR TURN

Use the space below to write out your own prayers and declarations.

FORM COVENANT FRIENDSHIPS

Scripture

Iron sharpens iron, so a man sharpens the countenance of his friend.

—Proverbs 27:17

This is My commandment, that you love and unselfishly seek the best for one another, just as I have loved you. No one has greater love [nor stronger commitment] than to lay down his own life for his friends.

—John 15:12–13, AMP

Now we who are strong [in our convictions and faith] ought to [patiently] put up with the weaknesses of those who are not strong, and not just please ourselves. Let each one of us [make it a practice to] please his neighbor for his good, to build him up spiritually.

—Romans 15:1–2, AMP

Carry one another's burdens and in this way you will fulfill the requirements of the law of Christ [that is, the law of Christian love].

—Galatians 6:2, AMP

Declarations

My friendships are not a coincidence; God has placed these women in my life for a reason.

I will commit myself to my friends and to forming deep and God-honoring friendships with them.

I will carry my friends' burdens.

When God shows me a good friend for me, I will commit to her as Ruth did to Naomi.

I will allow the Lord to use my friendship and loyalty to bring about good in the lives of my friends.

I will do my part to "sharpen" my friends, and I will be open to them doing the same for me (Prov. 27:17).

I will lay down my life for my friends (John 15:12–13).

I will stand with my friends through adversity.

PRAYERS

Lord, I ask that You make me into a covenant friend. I believe that one can chase a thousand and two can put ten thousand to flight. In covenant friendships there is exponential power to accomplish more in the kingdom. Lord, bring women into my life that we may have agreement in our faith. I believe that there is power in agreement. Agreement and unity attracts Your presence. I ask that You will bring divine connections and friendships into my life. I believe two are better than one. Send loyal women into my life, women who love me for who I am and not what I can give them. Lord, Your Word says, "Greater love has no man than this, that a man lay down his life for his friends" (John

15:13, RSV). *I ask that You would make me into a selfless friend. Teach me how to serve others and place others' needs before my own.*

Lord, release a new expression of teamwork among women. Let women understand that together we can accomplish more for Your glory. I break the spirit of discord and confusion among women. We will rise up and declare that we can do more together than we can do separately. These are the days in which every woman will find her rank and column in the army of the Lord. We will not push or compete, but we will support and encourage each of our sisters in her destiny.

Your Turn

Use the space below to write out your own prayers and declarations.